Harmonious

Wishes,

A. Turpeau

678-522-6548

The Harmonious Way™

A Success Guide to Selecting A Compatible Mate

By

Aaron Turpeau, Ph.D.

Pantheo, Inc.
Reno, Nevada 89501

More Praise for
The Harmonious Way

"Turpeau's *The Harmonious Way* is a very effective method for improving your relationship with yourself and with others, and for providing deep and lasting emotional healing."

Therman Evans, M.D., Author/Lecturer Phila., PA

"*The Harmonious Way* will lift your spirits and force you to take a look inside your soul to bring forth the best you have to offer."

Black Elegance Magazine– New York, NY

"*The Harmonious Way* will help you evaluate your expectations of marriage to make sure they align with God's plan for husband and wife."

African American Parent Magazine, Detroit, MI

"Do you believe in magic? Do you see love relationships as a mystical power that is totally irresistible and impossible to control? If you do, and go into a relationship on that basis, the odds are high that it will at worst end in tragedy or be a tremendous disappointment. Dr. Turpeau's *The Harmonious Wa y* will help you to make intelligent choices when consider- ing who will share your favor."

Chandler-White Publishing, Chicago, IL

"Given the disturbing number of failed relationships, this book is timely, practical, thought provoking and down right-honest. I loved it."

Judge Glenda Hatchett, Host,
nationally syndicated TV show- *Judge Hatchett*
Atlanta, GA

To Michelle Wallace Turpeau,
the love of my life.

Acknowledgements

I am in a place of deep gratitude when I think about all of the love and support that has been given to me by my family, friends and colleagues. They have allowed me to play my true note and follow my calling. Many thanks to:

Colleagues
Charles Josey, for his excellent writing skills and assistance in developing this text;

Jean Ross, radio personality and host of the *Mid-Day Atlanta Live* program on AM 1380 WAOK- Atlanta, GA, for inviting me to be a frequent guest on her talk program.

Family and Friends
My parents, Brenda and Aaron Turpeau, Sr., for supporting me in many ways and always believing in me;

My wife, Michelle Turpeau, for everything, particularly sacrificing and supporting a husband following his dream;

My brother, Michel Turpeau and his family, and sister Alem Turpeau, for being there in many ways to help out when needed;

My kids, Micah, Blake and Brooke, for being my motivation to do more, and for opening my heart to dimensions of Love previously unknown;

Roland Lane, Jr. and Vera Taylor, for encouragement and proofreading.

Finally, I want to thank all of the people who have been my counseling and seminar clients in the past and whose names and other identifying information were changed for the purposes of this book. Because of the examples you set in the past and your willingness to live harmoniously I am able to write this book with authority. May this work bring others closer to the Holy.

To God be the glory.

Table of Contents

Introduction

Is This Book for You?

Have you ever sat at a piano and struck a single note? Any note on the keyboard sounds good by itself. The more additional notes you strike, the more complex the sound. When compatible notes are added, the harmony they create is pleasing, enjoyable, exciting. However, certain additions can grate on the nerves because all notes are not in harmony with one another. Interestingly enough, a note that clashes with one is a perfect companion for other notes on the keyboard. It's the combinations that matter; it's the combinations that either blend or irritate.

People are like that. Some are in harmony with you; some aren't. And, there is little you can do to change life's harmonics; you simply learn to choose notes that harmonize with yours. Many people have trouble achieving harmony in their lives because they aren't exactly certain what their individual note is. Once they learn it and sound it loud and clear, others that harmonize will ring out in response.

That's the way it was meant to be, and learning to accept and use this law of nature to your advantage can make an incredible difference in every aspect of your life. You don't have to alter your note in order to harmonize; you don't have to fake a sound that isn't yours. The goal of this book is to help you find, accept, and sound your note in a way that pleases you and draws to you the conditions and people who can make your life a satisfying and much richer experience. If that's what you are looking for, please read on; this book was written for you.

I call learning to accept and use this natural law *The Harmonious Way*^TM. It is a path you can successfully follow in several aspects of your life. While, most of the book focuses on finding a love partner who is right for you, you can also follow *The Harmonious Way* when selecting friends, when dealing with family, and when selecting your career or refocusing the one you now have. If, say, achieving harmony in your career or friendships is your sole reason for reading this book, I encourage you to read more than the section dedicated to the subject of chief interest to you. I make this recommendation because the chapter on career, friends, and family builds on the information and concepts covered in the earlier chapters. So, I hope you will read it all and in sequence, in order to get the big picture, concerning where *The Harmonious Way* can lead you.

One more thing I would like to mention up front is, with the exception of the authorities I have quoted and the members of my family, all names in this book have been changed out of respect for the privacy of individuals.

Now, let's start finding the harmonies for your life's note.

Defining The Harmonious Way

The Harmonious Way. What is it? It is the path through life that can help you experience the peace and harmony you want and deserve. Through your love relationship, you can have the life qualities that matter most to you. *The Harmonious Way,* which respects you and your desires, is an approach to expanding your life and achievement. However, it is not a singular path for all of us to march down. Rather it is multiple individual paths, one for each of us. This book's aim is to set you on the one with your name on it, a path on which you can live your life out loud, not compromising who you are.

There are dozens of books and TV shows that sell the idea that, before you can find happiness in a relationship, you must first become happy with yourself. Well, that is at least partially true; however, it's a perspective that tends to be unrealistic and misleading. Here is why. The pain of loneliness alone can prevent you from being happy with the person you are. Consequently a vicious, self-destructive cycle can develop, instead of the happy one you long to achieve. On the other hand, *The Harmonious Way* recognizes that progress in multiple areas can take place simultaneously.

We human beings are social animals, not isolated organisms that live in private vacuums and work, work, work on themselves until they are happy. Another reason the concept of being happy with yourself first is misleading and counterproductive is that it promotes the idea that there is some state of being for which you must strive and reach. A final destination. And, only after you get there, can you say, "At last I am happy with who I am. Finally, I am allowed to pursue a meaningful love relationship, career or whatever I wish."

Well, life just doesn't work that way. We have good days and bad days, good moods and bad moods. There is hardly ever a continued state of happiness. Therefore, if you take this sequential approach, you are in danger of getting stuck in a rut, never creating the reality of love that you so strongly desire and deserve.

The morsel of truth in the sequential concept is, if you want a lasting love relationship, rewarding career, and compatible friends, you do need to focus on yourself first. However, the goal is not some state of continuous happiness and perfection that functions as a magnet, drawing all you want from life to you. No. What can help you the most is an increased awareness of the person you really are. Discovering ourselves is a process that lasts a lifetime. I believe, if you take into account what you already intuitively know about yourself and accept who you are, you can find someone to share your life, someone who is in harmony with the real you. The same is true for friends and career. However, at this point, set aside the issues of friendship and career, and let's focus on the issue of a life partner for you.

In order to find a lasting love relationship, you must first become willing to be yourself. You must become willing to sound your own note. That means taking time out to discover who you really are and being honest with yourself, concerning your findings. This book is a practical guide that can lead you to that discovery. It doesn't thump the Bible, but it is written with a down to earth spirituality that "keeps it real."

The Harmonious Way for relationship shopping and maintenance respects your individuality and does not ask you to give up who you are in order to have a love partner. It merely asks you to discover the note that you were created to express and then produce that note loud and clear. If you join up with another note and the music is not pleasing to your soul's ear, then you need to move on and find another note that will blend with yours to produce beautiful music. That's *The Harmonious Way*, the path I invite you to travel.

"The ruin of a nation begins in the homes of its people."

Ghanaian Proverb

Chapter 1

Finding and Keeping a Love Partner

It was half past midnight on a November night in Los Angeles County, California. I found myself on the cold bathroom floor, staring through tears at my vomit in the toilet. Another one of my love relationships had failed, and this time, I was breaking up with my first wife. I was hurt, bewildered, and filled with gnawing questions that I could not answer. "Why?" I cried out to God, "Why can't I find and keep a love partner?"

No answer came from outside me or from within. My anxiety and depression only produced a headache so severe that I felt as if I was about to snap away from the world of the sane. Suddenly, suicide seemed like a reasonable option. Scared by the fact that I was entertaining such thoughts, I went to a nearby hospital and, after talking to an empathetic counselor, found myself gradually regaining my sanity. Yes, I know what it feels like to ache for a partner's companionship, only to feel it slip through my fingers time and time again. The pain of a break up, which I, many others, and perhaps you have experienced, is not the only undesirable consequence from a relationship gone sour. Relationship breakups can have major consequences that tear at the very fabric of our society.

How many times have you been up late at night, having a discussion with family or friends about the various problems of society? Likely someone in the group theorized that one of the major causes of these problems is the breakdown of the family. It's really not a theory; it's a fact. Families are in a state of crisis, the divorce rate is at an all time high, and children are caught in the middle of parental wars.

Our values in America reflect that we are not as interested in the preservation of the family as we are with material gain and technological advancement. Our major goal, in the education system, is to produce human beings with technical skills that can keep the economic machine of America chugging along at an ever-quickening pace. Few voices lift up the value of character-building and interpersonal relationship training as legitimate goals of our school systems. With the advent of more and more school shootings, it seems that educational systems would see the handwriting on the wall and start recognizing the need for more than just the traditional methods of education. Our families are coming apart, and when this happens our national security is threatened from within.

Families would be much stronger if our marital relationships were stronger. Many marriages today suffer - not because of any innate faults or weaknesses in the individual parties involved but rather because there's a lack of harmony in the relationship. The partners involved in the marriage are not compatible. Each person in a love relationship is an expression of God and deserves to be valued as such. However, we must recognize that, just because we are all valuable creatures, this does not mean that we can all live under the same roof harmoniously. Oil and water are both valuable, but they don't mix. Cats and parrots are both God's creations; however, that does not mean He meant for them to share the same perch.

Trying to change your Self or someone else to make a relationship work is the way of disrespect. *The Harmonious Way* is the way of respect, and it entails accepting and respecting yourself and others. A compatible partner will let you implement your self-concept and also meet your relationship needs. For most people, the problem in moving ahead to the next step is that they're taking it before they learn who they are, and what they want from a relationship. Others make a slightly different mistake. After going through the self-discovery steps, they then try to force a particular person to give them what they need. You have the God given right to be the person you were created to be and to have your needs met. And so does everyone else. Each of you has a need to express the true Self within you, to sound your note, and enjoy the experience of being in harmony with a compatible love partner.

At this point, I want to begin showing you the route we will follow, in order to travel *The Harmonious Way* of finding a love partner who meets your needs. To reach your destination, you will need to learn the answers to some questions. Collectively they should take you to your destination: a love partner for life. In simplistic terms, *The Harmonious Way* is a five-segment process of learning to (1) be yourself, (2) examine yourself, (3) determine the type of environment or person who will allow you to be yourself, (4) find that environment or person, and (5) maintain the relationship. In other words, rather than changing who you are to fit other people's desires, you take inventory of yourself and discover who you are. You learn what note you were created to express. Once you get in touch with the person you are, what your desires in life are, and what you want from a partner in a love relationship, you will be well on your way to finding a love partner and building a relationship that can last.

You now know the identity of the five segments, which is not unlike knowing the names of five great works of art. And like great art, each time you look at the segments, you will see greater detail and additional meaning. Chapter by chapter, we will look deeper and deeper into how you go about experiencing The Harmonious Way. So, let's take our first look.

1. *How can I be my Self?* - This is the very first and the most important step to The Harmonious Way. This step requires you to have the courage to play your true note, to be genuine with yourself and with others. This may be scary for some, but the benefit is inner harmony. To force your Self to live harmoniously with others without inner harmony produces an artificial life. We must be true to our hearts.

2. *Who am I?* - Once you have started living a genuine life, you are then in a position to examine your revitalized Self and begin answering the question: Who am I? To arrive at the answer, you need to go on a mental safari to hunt down as much information as you can about yourself, enough to answer the following questions.

A. What am I like spiritually, physically, and emotionally?

B. How do I relate and communicate with other people?

C. What are my interests?

D. What is my personal financial attitude, and how important is financial wealth to me?

E. What are my goals in life?

F. What are my values?

G. How would I describe my personality?

H. How do I prefer spending my leisure time?

3. What type of person do I want my partner to be? - Rather than haphazardly waiting on cupid to romantically strike you with a glimpse of somebody you think is cute, why not sit down and seriously ask yourself the question above? Taking time out to really answer it can save you from a lot of unnecessary future heartaches.

4. How do I find a person who will allow me to be my Self and also meet my relationship needs? - This part explores some practical ways to actually find a good relationship for you instead of going back to your old unconscious patterns of searching and identifying potential partners. This part is designed to keep you from ever saying again, "Why do I always end up with dogs?"

5. How do I maintain a love relationship? - This section examines what it takes to make a relationship last. It is written based on my experience with couples who have and do not have long lasting, happy marriages. Keep in mind that long-lasting and happy do not necessarily go hand in hand. With that in mind, the next time you are in church and the pastor announces that Mr. and Mrs. Committed have been married for fifty years, go ahead and clap because it is a great achievement, no matter what anyone says. But, keep in mind not to be so quick to judge the quality of a marriage based on the length of years spent together. Two people can stay together for years; however, if they were not happy during those decades, then a sympathetic hug may be as justified as congratulatory applause.

"When will my reflection show who I am inside?"

Walt Disney's Mulan

Chapter 2

The Harmonious Way to Find Your Mate

Turpeau, I'm telling you man, girls want you to lie to them. You can't be honest!"

I clearly remember being told that one afternoon in a dormitory hall. It was during my college years, when a friend and I were theorizing about how to find girlfriends. I mentioned that I thought people should be themselves. After vehemently disagreeing with me, he saw that I was surprised. So, he went on to explain that he believed females look for certain things in a male. "If you're smart, Turpeau, you'll make them believe that you have each and every characteristic they're looking for - even if you don't have them."

I didn't argue with him, but he did provide me with food for thought. The more I considered his theory and attempted practicing it, the more I believed he was one hundred percent wrong. But, unfortunately, I didn't come to that conclusion before my first marriage. Like so many others, I was still trying to figure out what type of guy a female wanted, then fool the world into believing that I was that guy. For example, once, my first wife and I were having problems in our relationship, and I tried to please her by buying tickets to a rock concert of a band that I did not appreciate at all. However, I knew that she enjoyed their music. I went to the concert and found myself in the middle of a stadium filled with people who were dressed like the musicians. During the band's performance, like everyone else, I began dancing. I tried hard to act as if I was having a good time, but in the midst of my head bobbing, it occurred to me that I wasn't being genuine. I was smothering my true Self in an attempt to win the acceptance of my wife and the other people around me. The whole experience was just another pathetic attempt to convince myself that she and I could have a good relationship, despite our obvious incompatibility.

If you are struggling to meet someone to be your life partner but are having no luck, consider letting the world see the real you. I know it sounds scary, but think about it. Not doing this and establishing a relationship with someone, based on a false image of yourself, is quite dishonest. It sounds like a cliche, but go ahead; dare to be *you*. Some readers are no doubt saying, "If I show who I truly am, nobody will like me." When you start thinking this way, just remember, "Everybody hasn't met you yet." That may sound like cruel humor, but the statement is true and can prove to be a positive viewpoint in the relationship-shopping world.

For some reason, many people believe they must like and be liked by everyone they encounter. That's not being realistic. The world we live in is so diverse; we are bound to encounter people whom we have nothing in common with, people with completely different viewpoints on how life should be lived. So, when some people meet you, they will not like you. We might as well accept the reality. On the other hand, there are people who will like you and accept who you truly are. This second group of people wants to meet you; however, when you do meet them, don't expect them to be turned on by false advertising. The ones you want to meet are looking for the real you - not a fake somebody else. False advertising or hiding yourself in the relationship market is putting out bait to catch something that you will eventually regret catching. You and others on the market deserve to have someone with whom you are happy and compatible. Wouldn't you like to have a life partner with whom you could relax and be yourself, versus someone you have to constantly perform for in order to win love? Sure, you would. It's an Eden-like experience. And,

I am fortunate enough to have such an experience.

My wife, Michelle, and I met each other in 1990 and have been married since 1992. Her genuineness was one of the things that attracted me the most. We try to be honest with each other as much as possible and let our true feelings show. This takes a lot of courage because there are many times when honesty leads to hurt feelings and arguments. I actually prefer this Eden-like relationship because we strive to be naked and unashamed. Although it isn't always easy to be honest, the resulting level of intimacy is well worth the confrontations.

A relationship, such as this, is quite different from the relationship I had with my first wife. The two of us hardly ever argued. In fact, we were quite civil and polite toward each other. But underneath, we were both thoroughly miserable. I did everything I could think of to make the relationship work, to save the marriage. I was determined to make it work. I worked so hard on being a reasonable facsimile of the partner she wanted, I failed to see that underneath, she had little desire to be married to anyone remotely like the true me.

Eventually we went to counseling and tried a technique that's often promoted in my field of counseling. The technique recognizes two different roles in a relationship: the pursuer and the distancer. In the relationship with my first wife, I was the pursuer of intimacy; she was the distancer. The distancer is only comfortable with a limited level of intimacy. The pursuer is usually not happy with a low level of intimacy; so, the pursuer tries to increase the level. Unfortunately, the opposite happens. The more intimacy attempted, the more the distancer's level of discomfort is increased.

This theory appears to be quite valid; however, in practice, I found it quite inefficient. Couples are usually asked to solve their marital frustrations in the following manner. Pursuers are asked to pretend they don't want intimacy from the distancer. This tricks the distancer into thinking something is wrong; so, the distancer works to increase the intimacy level.

It did not work for me personally; however, during my early years as a counselor, I fell in step with my colleagues and promoted it with other couples who were having problems. Without fail, the technique generated only short-term favorable results. Here is why. In a relationship, people deserve to have the type of intimacy that they find comfortable. Rather than recognizing this, pursuers are asked not to be so needy and dependent. They are told to "get a life" or at least a hobby. Distancers are informed that they have intimacy problems, usually relating back to experiences they had growing up. There may be some truth to that, but the approach simply fails to respect where, at that particular time in their lives, the individuals are. Both pursuers and distancers are made to feel bad about themselves and feel that they are people with problems that only extensive psychotherapy could possibly cure. So, couples who sincerely try to play this game find that, like all games, it eventually has to come to an end. It had to end because it requires people to behave in a manner that cuts across the grain of who they are and smothers true feelings. Furthermore, it is a game in which there are no winners because both parties lose their self-respect. So, in the long run, pretending to be who you aren't goes against the natural self-actualizing tendency of the human organism.

The advantage of being honest with ourselves and with others is that we are more likely to end up with someone with whom we are truly compatible. If you do not want someone up under you 24-7, then find someone who has the same perspective. If you are very affectionate and demonstrative, find a person who matches your need for physical expression. There is love out there for you today! You do not have to waste your time trying to heal someone back to intimacy. Save that job for the counselors; let us take care of that. You don't have to try making someone ready for a committed relationship who isn't there. The hard truth is that person may never become ready for the type of committed relationship you need now. Again, let my colleagues and me handle those people. There are plenty of others out there who are ready, willing, and able to be in an intimate, committed relationship. Many ripe apples out there, waiting to be picked. Don't waste your life trying to change green apples and rotten apples into ripe ones.

Be genuine. Be the real person you are. When you do, people who are not compatible with you will be turned off, and that is a good thing. Yes, it is a very good thing. If you are searching for a partner, you do not need to have your time wasted by someone who is going to end up despising you. The best thing is to be yourself. Truthful advertising is essential. That way, the other person is aware of what he or she is getting into and won't end up in a counselor's office, saying what I have heard so many times before: "He changed on me."

If you are going to live your life with a partner, it should not be a relationship that requires you to work at being something you are not. We spend long hours at work. When we come home we want to let our hair down, take our shoes off, and be ourselves. Your partner in life should be one who can accept the real you. We don't want to have to work hard on our relationships when we come home. Relationships do require focused work, but it should be enjoyable work that fits who you are - not labor that requires you to march to a different drummer or bob your head to an unpleasant rhythm.

If you are in a relationship with a person who does not allow you to be who you are, then you have several choices:

A. *You can remain in your current predicament and just bear your burden of being unequally yoked to each other.*

B. *You can coerce the other person into artificially changing into an imitation of the person you need in your life.*

C. *You can artificially change and appear to be more to your partner's likings.*

D. *Both of you can find other partners with whom you have more in common.*

Just a hint, finding a person with whom you have many things in common is *The Harmonious Way.* It is the way that allows you to be real, sound your true note, and live out loud.

If the unconscious could speak, over and over we would likely hear, "I know what type of person I am, but I want a mate who is different." Or, "I don't have a clue concerning who I am, but I'm going after that person to be my partner in my life."

When we think and act like this, we turn mate selection into nothing more than a crapshoot. People spend more time planning their vacations than deciding who their life partner should be. The result: broken relationships, broken families.

Why not take the necessary time out to discover who you are? And then, based on the information, shop for a relationship wisely, rather than waiting on romance to whisk you way up high on an emotionally charged cloud of passion - only to drop you like a rock a short time later, causing you to land on hard reality. Only if we take the time out to discover who we are can we accept ourselves before tumbling into a relationship that leads to the sudden stop that awaits, when we fail to take *The Harmonious Way*. However, based on a clear understanding of who we are, each of us can shop for someone who is genuinely compatible. Just because someone is available, great looking, rich or famous, doesn't mean he or she is the one for you.

Taking time out to explore who we truly are and what we want from a mate is so important. Your mate can have a big influence on you and on whether or not you implement your self-concept. The amount of happiness a person obtains is proportionate to the degree to which that individual is able to implement her or his self concept, her or his true self. That's what *"playing your true note"* is all about. Choosing the wrong love partner can hinder you. We must take a serious look at whom we are dating and with whom we are considering having a long-term relationship. If we leave our mate choice up to fate and do not try to manage whom we end up with, then we are engaging in risky behavior that may develop into a lonely, unfulfilling, monotonous life. But, if we choose the path of *the Harmonious Way*, then we will find joy because we are not muted and are able to play our true note in a lilting, harmonic song of love.

"The most common form of despair is not being who you are."

Kierkegaard

Chapter 3

Start by Playing Your True Note

What is *Playing Your True Note?*

Playing your true note is "keeping it real." Being who you really are. Living a genuine life. A life that is not masked, smothered, closeted or ashamed. Not concealing who you really are requires great courage and faith. There is often a fear that humanity will reject us and intentionally or unintentionally hurt us. However, deep down we know that we must be who we are created to be. If we don't, we suffer consequences that manifest in physical or mental illness, or at least miserably unhappy lives.

> "Then the Lord God placed the man in the Garden of Eden to cultivate it and guard it. He told him, "You may eat the fruit of any tree in the garden, except the tree that gives you the knowledge of what is good and what is bad. You must not eat the fruit of that tree; if you do, you will die the same day.'...The man and the woman were both naked, but they were not embarrassed.... The woman saw how beautiful the tree was and how good its fruit would be to eat, and she thought how wonderful it would be to become wise. So she took some of the fruit and ate it. Then she gave some to her husband, and he also ate it. As soon as they had eaten it, they were given understanding and realized that they were naked; so they sewed fig leaves

together and covered themselves. That evening they heard the Lord God walking in the garden, and they hid from Him among the trees. But the Lord God called out to the man, 'Where are you?' He answered, 'I heard you in the garden; I was afraid and hid from you, because I was naked.' 'Who told you were naked?' God asked. 'Did you eat the fruit that I told you not to eat?'"

--Genesis Chapters 2 and 3 TEV

This ancient story amazes me each time I read it because it so powerfully comments on humanity's relationship with God. The writers did an excellent job of communicating why humanity suffers. Many times listeners, as well as readers of the story will emphasize different aspects of what is written. "Where exactly was this garden located?" "Adam and Eve disobeyed God, so God punished all of humanity." The one that puzzles me the most is the implication in today's culture that the fruit is symbolic of sexual intercourse.

I am not a creationist who demands that the story be interpreted literally. And, I am not an empiricist who completely discounts the story because of lack of physical evidence. This old debate, that surprisingly still occurs in some circles, saddens me because the two sides are so busy trying to prove the other wrong that I think they are missing out on a message from God that the writer of the story was trying to communicate to us.

I believe that through this biblical story, God is telling us our purpose in life does not include trying to figure out the difference between good and evil. The only thing that can come of doing that is the establishment of standards that people will inevitably fail to live up to. The more we become moral champions, telling ourselves and other people what is right and what is wrong, the more we eat from the tree that God did not intend for us to touch. The more we eat from this tree, the more we recognize that we do not measure up to the current societal standards; therefore, we are embarrassed. Our true Selves, our naked Selves, reveal who we really are. And, who we really are does not neatly fit into the picture of what society deems as acceptable. So, to avoid embarrassment we sew fig leaves to cover our naked Selves; we hide our true Selves in a figurative closet.

Whereas before we eat this fruit, we are with God and with each other, and we are not ashamed of who we are. I am I, and you are you. We are acceptable in God's sight. But, the more we eat of this fruit of what is good and what is bad, the more guilty we feel and our self-esteem and esteem for others declines as the fruit digests. This leaves us feeling bad about others, and ourselves.

To combat this guilty feeling, many choose to become experts of the moral law, like the Pharisees during the time of Jesus. We can tell everyone what is pleasing to God and what is not pleasing to God. I used to be one of those Christian Pharisees. I set out in my Christian development to become a moral champion and worked very hard at discerning what was good and what was evil. I also felt it was my duty to share with others what the Bible had to say about certain behaviors and what people needed to do to get right with God. You have probably met many people like the old me, and you may even recognize that you have some Pharisee in you, as well.

As we observe history, we see that the spirit of the Pharisees has been around a long time. This pharisaic spirit is no respecter of persons; it doesn't care what religion, nationality, gender, sexual orientation, political party, or social status you are. Disciples of the Bible must agree that Jesus was more upset with the Pharisees than any other group of people. This spirit doesn't just exist in the religious world. There are moral crusaders in all walks of life. You can recognize them as people (liberal or conservative) who act as if they have the corner on the market of knowledge, concerning how human beings should think, feel, and act.

So, we walk the walk and talk the talk, hoping that our true naked Selves will never be exposed, out of fear that we may be labeled weirdo, freak, low class, or sinful. Eating from the tree of the knowledge of good and evil has alienated us from God and each other. We know what is acceptable and unacceptable, and we hide our Selves because we are scared of condemnation from God and from others. If we could hear our unconscious thoughts they would probably say, "If other people really knew me, they would not accept me." "God knows me, and I know that I am unacceptable in God's sight, I'll just not think about God until Sunday morning. I'll go sit in the back of church, be on my best behavior, pay my tithes, and ask for forgiveness." Our fear of rejection keeps us cloaked, hiding our true Selves.

Once, when my four-year-old daughter and I were at home alone, I was downstairs in my basement doing some work. Suddenly, I heard a man's voice upstairs. I quickly looked up and saw the yard guy was coming down the stairs to talk to me. Right behind him was my daughter. I was flustered and furious but quickly gathered myself to talk to the yard guy. After he left, I laid heavy into my daughter with reprimands and warnings for her not to ever let someone in the house again. She clearly got the message that this was not the appropriate thing for her to do, and as her eyes began to well up, you could see that she began to take it personally and was hurt. All of a sudden, she ran to her room, shut and locked the door behind her. In essence she put herself in a closet.

I taught her the difference between right and wrong. I felt that this lesson was necessary, but it did come with a price. For that moment, she did not want her soul to be known because she was ashamed of it. We do not want to be exposed to others when we feel we are being or will be negatively evaluated by others. Therefore, we shut ourselves in closets and lock the door so that others will not know us. We do not want others to see that we do not fit the ideal or standard set for us. That standard society uses to measure our worth. That standard used to declare us good or bad.

Outside of her bedroom door, that day, I recognized that I had caused my daughter's soul to hide from me. I felt like God calling for a hidden Adam in the garden. I was finally able to convince her to open the door and then decided to take a different approach. We role-played and practiced her answering the door and telling the guest that she has to get one of her parents. I also tried to more calmly and respectfully explain why it was very important for her not to let people into the house. From this experience, I not only learned that I needed a louder doorbell, but I also learned that it is necessary to teach certain desired behavior for various reasons; however, the challenge is to do so in a manner that salvages the dignity and worth of the individual.

Ironically, even though we earnestly try to keep our Selves clothed in righteousness, we cannot deny the deep urge within us to express our true nature. We want to be known and accepted by others. So, we seek attention and approval from the world. To our puzzlement, although the attention is nice, it proves unsatisfying. It's unsatisfying because the person we present is not our true and complete Self. We do this and still wonder why we have such a deep sense of loneliness.

I remember Melissa, a freshman at a university. While she was growing up, she held fast to the idea that to grow up means to graduate from high school and go away to college. So, here she was out of state, proving to her Self and to the people back home that she had indeed grown up. There was only one problem. She was miserable.

From the moment Melissa arrived on campus, she worked hard to make friends. She tried going out to parties, meeting people, drinking, joining a sorority, joining clubs. Although she was friendly toward everyone she met and was always smiling, for some strange reason she had a hard time fitting in. On the outside, Melissa seemed very happy. You would not have known how miserable and lonely she felt.

Melissa came to counseling to sort out her feelings of being homesick and receive help in trying to decide whether or not to transfer to a university close to her hometown. During counseling, Melissa went back home one weekend. She was very close to her family and friends back there and had a wonderful time. For those two days, all of her loneliness was replaced with joy. When she returned to school, her misery also returned.

It seems that since she was so unhappy she would just transfer; however it wasn't that easy. There was a big obstacle in the way. Melissa held a belief that came from an unstated principle in her family. That belief was that to grow up, you must go away to college. Believing that, she was not allowing the true Melissa to live and breathe, to return home and express who she was. Eventually, counseling helped her debunk her irrational belief and allowed her to transfer back home.

I guess some therapist would have tried to make Melissa fight her homesickness in the name of individuation or some other theoretical dynamic, but I did not see that as necessary. I honestly suspect that Melissa already had her mind made up as to what she really wanted to do, but she just needed someone to give her permission to be who she really is. She needed her inner Self to be affirmed and not be labeled as an immature baby.

A couple of months after she transferred, I received a postcard from Melissa saying that she was enjoying being at her hometown university and that everything was going well. She had made friends, was making good grades, and was much happier. While the old pre-transfer Melissa looked perfectly happy and normal on the outside, I suspect that the smile of the post-transfer Melissa has a more authentic gleam.

How many people do we know in our lives who seem to live perfectly normal and happy lives? It could be that they are the loneliest people. Lonely because the persona they present to the world is one that is very conventional and acceptable, a persona that makes no significant impression. They win the acceptance of others, but it is shallow. Therefore, they remain lonely deep down, wanting to express who they really are. In the words of E.E. Cummings,

> *To be nobody but myself, in a world which is doing its best, night and day, to make you everybody else means to fight the hardest battle any human being can fight, and never stop fighting.*

How Do I Play My True Note?

As we grow, it's expected that we go through a process known as individuation. This process is fueled by an instinct within that directs us toward self-fulfillment and wholeness. It is the process of self-actualization. During this process you must separate yourself from the collective and discover your own way.

Some of us cooperate more with this process than others. The more you cooperate with it the more you are able to be who you were created to be. Growing up is not an easy process because the child is usually dependent on and hopefully obedient to the parents. This is normal and ideal in order for that child to become a healthy, respectful, and responsible person within society. However, as we grow older, we become less dependent and obedient because the need for these types of parent-child dynamics decreases.

Unfortunately, some parents want their offspring to maintain the same level of dependence and obedience, no matter how old they become. This gets in the way of the individuation process. The interference of parents can cause much stress in the lives of their sons and daughters. People try to have fulfilling, whole lives in the areas of their careers and their love relationships, but parents can often be the saboteurs of the natural process.

In the midst of this strong filial press, it's the individual's job to assertively stand up for his or her Self. If you want to have harmony in your life, then as you grow up, you must also grow out. You must become who you truly are. Warning!! This will often lead to many knock-down, drag-out arguments between you and your parents or others who want to keep you in your so-called "place." Nonetheless, if you stand firm and remain respectful in the midst of disrespect for your inner Nature, then you will eventually gain the respect of those who criticize and wish to control you.

I am reminded of Eldridge, who came from a very well-to-do family. His mother was an accomplished surgeon, and his father a successful businessman. At college, when Eldridge met and fell in love with Felicia, the two of them developed a great relationship. There was, however, one problem. Felicia came from a low socioeconomic class, and this was just not acceptable to Eldridge's parents. They were socialites who belonged to all the right clubs, and they spent a great deal of intentional effort to make sure that Eldridge was exposed to the "right" kind of peers. When they met Felicia, they treated her with respect, but they were truly disappointed when they learned of her background.

Though Eldridge's parents were disappointed, they decided not to worry about their son's love interest, hoping that it would eventually pass.

However, Eldridge's and Felicia's love for each other only grew. Then one day, Eldridge informed his parents that he and Felicia were engaged. According to Eldridge, his parents were stunned by the news and looked at each other as if they were telepathically communicating, "Red Alert!! Red Alert!!"

Eldridge's parents began trying to convince him that marriage was not a good idea for him at this point in his life. He disagreed. When the real reason for their disapproval was revealed, Eldridge and his parents had several blowout arguments, concerning his relationship with Felicia. Then the parents played their trump card; they threatened to cease supporting him financially, if he continued his relationship with her.

At first, Eldridge bravely stood up to his parents, but the practicality of his parents' financial support strongly influenced his marriage plans. Eldridge persuaded Felicia that they should put off their marriage plans until much later. They also decided to hide their relationship from his parents. These new decisions created much stress in the relationship and eventually led to its demise.

All of the above brought Eldridge to me, as a client. He is now in his thirties, hopping from relationship to relationship, with none of them lasting for more than a few months. He told me that, when he was with Felicia, he was more stable and focused on his career goals. Now he can't really focus on anything, regarding his career or otherwise, because his need for intimacy is dominant. He has lost touch with Felicia, but the last he heard she was married with children. Eldridge is mad at himself for not having the courage to be his own person and not continuing his relationship with Felicia - despite his parents' disapproval. He gets along with his mother and father, but in our sessions together, his resentment toward them often surfaces. He says that his parents pressure him to settle down and establish a career. I haven't talked to his parents, but I have often wondered if they recognize that, in their attempt to protect their son, they may have contributed to the delaying of his realization of a happy and whole life. Sometimes the road to hell on earth is paved with good intentions.

Why Should We Play Our True Note?

When we do not express who we are, the lack of expression gradually destroys us. Unexpressed being can be physically and emotionally immobilizing, and harm our health, relationships and thinking. We are all souls that have appeared in the flesh, to live out our calling from God. When we do not genuinely express ourselves, we do not answer His call. There is a price to pay for not heeding this call.

Whatever may be our reason for not living out our calling, be it unacceptable to society or our own internal fears, the consequence of this unexpressed being is the quenching of our Holy Spirit within. Sounding our own priceless note is the only answer to the consequences that will keep the fires of the Spirit going.

My daughter, Micah, often is given dolls for presents. After she takes them out of the box, the clothes always come off in a matter of minutes, and the doll's clothes spend the rest of eternity in the bottom of her toy box. Our house looks like a doll nudist colony. One day when my daughter was three, a great aunt of mine asked Micah why her dolls had no clothes on? She replied, "So they can be more comfortable."

I suggest to you that this is also the reason why we should come out of our righteous clothing. It's very uncomfortable, stifling your true note, wearing masks, and putting on fronts. It's uncomfortable because this behavior cuts against the grain of who we are. It's uncomfortable because the Universe is trying to tell us that we should be cooperating with our calling and bliss. And, it's uncomfortable because it's lonely.

Have you ever noticed that many successful comedians tend to be very honest about topics we would never approach with such candor? We may not agree with what they are saying, but we often find it entertaining to listen to them. We listen, not just because they are funny, but also because we find their honesty so refreshing. Often, we admire the comic for saying what we always wanted to say but never had the guts to express ourselves. We vicariously enjoy taking the clothes off of humanity and exposing our true nature.

There are many social gatherings I find quite boring because no one is different and genuine. I must admit that I am not too genuine in these settings either. It's scary taking your clothes off when everyone else is clothed. There have been settings, however, when I have courageously been myself, in spite of the individuals who were cloaked and closeted around me. At first, honesty shocks them, and they don't know quite how to react. But, usually they become more relaxed and feel like they also can reveal who they really are. I have often times, in church, class, at work, or other social settings, dared to be myself in these hostile environments. I say hostile because they tend to be environments that intimidate us into staying within our closets, not daring to live our lives out loud. However, when I do dare to be my self in these environments, someone usually comes up to me and says, "I am so glad you said that!" Or "I am so glad you did that!" They usually report that they wanted to say or do something similar but lacked the courage. They also feel like a big burden is lifted when they see or hear someone else being genuine. It gives them permission to be themselves. It is contagious. However, even if we do not express ourselves, it can still be frightening when someone else dares to do so. Still, we usually find ourselves privately cheering for the brave soul who dared to be heard, to live out loud, sounding his or her true note. We vicariously share in their joy of liberty, wishing we could experience this freedom, as well.

We owe it to our creator to be who we were created to be. If we want to define sin as an offense against God, then not to cooperate with the sacred flow of our lives could be considered sinful because this behavior offends the God within. The wages of this type of sin is death of Self.

Obstacles to Playing Your True Note

The only thing intolerable is intolerance. We need to learn to accept diversity and allow others to be who they are. Some may respond, "But what they want to be is sinful."

Really? How do we know that just because something is different or unacceptable in our eyes, it is sinful? Is your answer "Because it goes against the Bible and what I was taught in church about God's will?" That's certainly the stock answer. The Bible has had a tremendous influence over our culture. We have benefited from this influence, but its influence has also caused problems.

There is a strong belief, that the Bible is the infallible Word of God, and whatever is written in that book can be interpreted to give us guidance to live our lives properly in the ambiguous world we inhabit.

This belief is so strongly promoted that anyone questioning it can be quickly ostracized by his or her community.

There is an old song you may know called "Gimme That Ol' Time Religion." It has a lyric that says, "It was good for my dear mother - it's good enough for me." Contrary to this song, maybe old time religion isn't good enough for us today. The melody to the song is quite pleasing, and it conjures up pleasant memories, but it promotes a mindset that refuses to change with new information.

There is a dynamic going on today in all types of religious communities, be they Christian, Muslim, Buddhist, Bahai, Judaism, or other religious communities. The religions themselves have great value, but many of the practitioners practice literalism. Literalists of any religion believe their scriptures and teachings are to be taken at face value and make no attempt at trying to interpret the deeper symbolic meaning. So, these people are living in the 21st Century and trying to literally live life by a collection of ancient writings.

Let us imagine that I went to Atlanta, Georgia and I had a map of the town that was drawn a hundred years ago. While using it to find my way, I become hopelessly lost. When you see me, you ask if I need help? I reply, "No, thank you; I have the map."

You see the map and discover that it's a century old. What would you say to me? You would probably try to explain to me that even though some of the main streets are the same, the city has changed drastically. Imagine your surprise when I say to you, "I have faith in this map, my great, great grandfather used this map, and it helped him get through town; therefore, it's good enough for me. As a matter of fact, you should make a copy of this map so you won't get lost, leaning on your own understanding." I don't know about you, but if I had an experience like that, I would walk away with my mouth dropped wide open in sheer amazement.

One of the best things that ever happened to me was going to seminary. It was there that I studied the Bible seriously and in depth. Studying the Bible is more than reading it from cover to cover and listening to pastors and teachers interpret. It is more than going through workbooks and reading commentaries. I challenge you to study the history of the Bible, and the literary structure of the writings (which by the way is quite impressive). Study the different cultures in which the Bible was written. This type of study will help put the Bible in perspective

My perspective of the Bible changed from viewing it as the unquestionable authority on God's will for everyone in all eons to viewing it as God inspired literature. It is surely splendid writing that is quite informative and inspiring for our own development. This may dishearten some to hear this perspective of the Bible, and I may be labeled as a backsliding sinner that was doomed by seminary. But, I must come out and speak my subjective truth. To do otherwise would lack integrity and would be a slap in the face to my Inner God.

The whole reason for this excursion into our perspective of the Bible and its place in our society is the Bible and the Church are often instruments of intolerance, rather than instruments of Grace. People do not feel free to be themselves in most church communities. These communities are full of events and fellowship that are filled with "appropriate" behavior. All the right words are said. The best foot is put forward. Men wear uncomfortable ties, and women wear uncomfortable shoes. Loving couples show little affection for each other, and the most foul-mouthed members are strangely mute.

One question: for whom is this show? The other members see and hear us outside of the church grounds. They know the more genuine you. When we go to church, it's as if we have stepped on Holy Ground where we must obey certain rules or be labeled an evil person. How many times have you gone to church and, upon returning home, you felt as if you had just been to work? It is like a place where we go to be as phony as we can be. If anything, it should be a place where we can be as real as we can be. A place where we can praise God and allow our Inner God to so shine before others that they may see our works and glorify our God within. But suffice it to say at eleven on Sunday mornings around this great land of ours, people are clothing their naked Selves and hiding from God during a time designated to commune with God in nakedness and truth. It is only when we are nakedly true to who we are that we are living in harmony with our Creator.

Helpful Characteristics for Playing Your True Note

The following is a list of characteristics that are beneficial to any person desiring to play their true note and find their true Selves.

Self-knowledge and Acceptance. Many of us need to spend enough quiet time with ourselves, listening to the voice of our Inner God, in order to discover who we are. The first step is to discover who that Self is and what does that Self really value?

In the movie based on the book *The Education of Little Tree*, an elderly man tells his grandson that the boy needs a secret place. Just like the character in this movie, we all need a secret or quiet place and time to center ourselves in order to get in touch with our God, who is within. Our children would probably fare better if we encouraged them to establish a quiet space and time to explore their inner world, too, a place away from media distractions, where they might discover and accept themselves. Discovery and acceptance of who we are is a gradual, constant process that needs to occur on a regular basis.

Once you find out who you are, the next step is *not* announcing your findings to the world. Rather, it is to *accept* who you are. Accepting ourselves is a necessary step. If you are a square peg, then you need to accept that fact and stop trying to fit in round holes. Many of us have a hard time accepting who we are and try to be something we are not. Whenever we do this, we head down dead end streets, traveling routes that lead to frustration... or to nowhere. Whereas if we accept who we are, it is more probable that we will have a smoother journey and a more successful life.

If we discover who we are but do not accept ourselves, we end up trying to be like other people. This is often manifested in career development. For example, let's say that deep down, you are really a great business executive or doctor but you are trying to be a football player or singer. Or, you are a writer, trying to be a business executive. Or a scholar, trying to be a runway model. Fame and fortune are often seductive. Just as it is fine to pursue a round hole if I am a round peg, it is fine to pursue the glamorous careers if they are a good fit for who you are. If I am not round and forcing my self to fit in a round hole, then I am setting myself up for frustration and failure. Even if I succeed and hammer myself into the round hole that doesn't fit, I create a very tight and uncomfortable situation, causing much stress and strain on my soul. This approach is the exact opposite of *The Harmonious Way*.

Role models create a dynamic that works against being who we are. And yet, we promote role modeling as the answer to helping our youth today. As a result, the media focuses on personalities and gives the public what it asks for. However, it is inevitable that, with the extreme amount of attention these role models receive, it is only a matter of time before the whole person is revealed rather than just the parts we like. Once we see the parts we don't like, we are extremely disappointed and do an about face in our allegiance to the famed personality. Then we start our search over, clamoring for that positive role model that we think we so desperately need.

The problem with the role model is that it asks our children to be like Mike, rather than be themselves. So many of our youngsters try to emulate their role models, whether they are entertainers, politicians, ministers, athletes, or other wealthy, respected, or beautiful people in the community. This sets the young up for failure. Trying to be someone else takes us away from discovering and accepting who we truly are. Sure, it's fine to hold a great scientist's accomplishments up as admirable - as long as you stop there and don't suggest that the young should model their whole being on the person. While the great scientist's accomplishments may be commendable, his personal life might not be. That, however, does not detract from the value of his scientific achievements. The same can be said of athletes and any other high achievers.

Courage. Even if you know and accept who you are, you also need courage. Many people know that they need to change their behavior but are afraid to do so. They are convinced that the positives outweigh the negatives. Still, they cannot bring themselves to the point where they are willing to suffer possible consequences. Public humiliation and not being accepted by others - especially rejection by people who are close or important to them - is greatly feared. Deep down we want to all be liked and accepted. To do something that will possibly cause someone to dislike us is asking a lot.

So, where does one find the courage that one needs to play one's true note? After one is convinced that playing his or her true note is best, one needs the courage to leap. This is definitely a leap of faith. If you do suffer negative consequences, which you probably will, how will you cope with them? Do you have what it takes to cope with these consequences? Many conclude that they don't and decide to keep their note muted. This is okay. This process is not for the weak of heart or the timid. It's for the courageous and takes a courage that is based on faith. Faith in whatever your belief system deems as trustworthy, be it yourself, others, God, your resources, your Self or anything else you ultimately depend on. It is not a faith that believes you will suffer no consequences, rather it is a faith that bravely asserts that whatever the consequences, the process and/or outcome will be good - or at least acceptable.

High Self-esteem. When playing your true note, it's extremely helpful to have high self-esteem because it gives you a shield, one that's strong enough to withstand attacks from without. If you depend on others' evaluation of you as a good or a bad person, then the thought of playing your true note will more then likely prove to be terrifying for you. However, if your self-esteem is based on your own perspective, then you are probably more prepared for the adventure ahead. In psychology, we use the term *locus of evaluation*. If your locus of evaluation is external, it means you depend on others to evaluate your worth. If your locus of evaluation is internal, then you evaluate your own worth. The latter condition is probably more ideal for the soul that wishes to sound out and express its being.

High achievers are often motivated by trying to please others. Many times it can be a vicious cycle that starts in childhood and, for many, continues throughout adulthood. Being successful early in life and receiving a great deal of praise can bring this on. The praise becomes addictive because it is so pleasing to the ego.

The child entertainer, chess champion, star athlete, and star scholar taste "success" at an early age and receive extreme praise for their performance. Unfortunately, their performance is associated with their feelings of self worth. As a star child grows older, he or she discovers that there are other star children, as well; he or she is not the only one. Therefore, the former child star no longer sees himself or herself as shining as brightly as originally assumed. This becomes very distressing, and he or she pathetically tries to maintain the attention and praise that was once received in younger years.

Unconditional, positive self-esteem is the key to having enough courage to play our true note out loud. We must be able to live out who we are, and if someone doesn't like it, we must have the ability to say "tough!" This takes tremendous self-esteem and it is admirable when viewed on a talk show or in people we meet. They may be putting up a brave front and actually be scared to death, but this brave behavior is still admirable because it takes even more courage to do something in the midst of extreme fear.

I commend any person who will stand up and say, "This is who I am." Many say that we are in need of heroes today. These people are, in a sense, heroes. They have answered the call from their Creator and have bravely expressed themselves. Each time we witness this, it is inspiring - even if we think that the person is misled or totally off base in their behavior or beliefs. We cannot deny the courage that is being displayed before us in the midst of a threatening environment. The difference between a hero and a model is, it takes great courage to do what the hero does. Courage doesn't necessarily come into play where models are concerned.

Patience. Lastly, patience is required. It takes patience and mercy to play your true note, a process that, for some, may need to be gradual because it can be scary. We have to learn to be patient with ourselves. And forgiving. There may be times when you look back at a situation that you know you did not handle with the courage or integrity you should have. But, that's okay. It took us many years to muffle our notes; so, if we don't suddenly express ourselves at full volume, then that's understandable. The main thing is not to be too hard on ourselves and to allow ourselves time to ease up on the soft peddle and ring out our individual notes loud and crystal clear. If you were not genuine in a particular situation, just say to your self, "Next time I will handle the situation in a better, more forthright way."

True Note Exercises

Self-knowledge. One way to go about acquiring greater self-knowledge is through a value clarification exercise taught to me by Dr. Steve Brown at the University of Georgia. Try this exercise. First list five things that you consider really important to you and who you are.

1. _____
2. _____
3. _____
4. _____
5. _____

The next step is for you to sit back and relax. Close your eyes. (I always find the eye closing part hard to do while I am reading a book). Let's say you listed family as one of your values. Now, imagine never having family in your life again for the rest of your days. As you are imagining this, experience the feelings that you are having. If the feelings are strongly negative, then you know that this is a strong value for you. You can do the same for all of the values you listed in order to help yourself prioritize which are more important to you. The values that it would hurt most to lose are the ones that matter most the to you. The others, while still important, are not as important. Knowing how you prioritize your values can be a tremendous help to you, if you are having a hard time focusing on what you want most out of life.

Courage Builders. Courage builders are like little baby steps toward sounding your true note. These are minor incidents that allow us to be ourselves in little ways. Saying "no" to certain requests that people make from you is an example. Make it a point to say "no" at least once to someone this week. If you don't feel like going to church this Sunday, don't go. And if someone asks you why you didn't, be prepared to honestly say you didn't feel like going. If you don't like the way your food is prepared in a restaurant, politely send it back. If a group of people is talking unfavorably about a movie, book, food item or something else that you truly like, then tell them that you like it. If we take these small opportunities to demonstrate courage, we will learn that we can take more and more chances at exposing who we truly are.

Self-esteem Savers. We can build our self-esteem in many ways. The best one is through our spiritual development and recognition of our Self. Yes, that's a major task; however, there are little everyday things that we can do to save our esteem from external assaults. We can avoid allowing others to evaluate us. This can be accomplished by not looking for praise or criticism from others. Don't ask people if they like your hair, your clothes or your work of art. The reason you are doing this is to save your self-esteem from becoming more and more easily affected by the negative or positive views of people you encounter. Instead, you want to empower your Self to evaluate you and not be dependent on others to keep your self-esteem tank filled. There is great power in having independent self-esteem. So, the next time you are criticized, just move on. And the next time you are praised, simply say "thank-you" and, again, move on. Neither praise nor criticism is that valid because anything praised by one person will be criticized by another. Just live your life as you see fit.

You Cannot Sound Another Person's Note

If you feel someone's true Self merits expression, talk to that person. Share your feelings on the subject. Then, leave it up to the individual to deal with the matter in his or her own way, without any stated or implied threat of doing the job for them. Threats amount to blackmail. Inner peace can not be thrust upon another; it must be sought and found within.

"You can never find yourself until you face the truth."

Pearl Bailey

Chapter 4
Who Am I?

Know Your Self

The next step in *The Harmonious Way* is Self-knowledge. After you choose to live a genuine life by being who you truly are, you will gradually feel the positive effects of living with inner harmony. Then it's time to get to know this real you, the inner person you are resurrecting from the living dead. This means you must become consciously aware of your Self, and that calls for more quiet time. You will be amazed by what you discover and what you can do with this knowledge. Self-knowledge is a powerful tool that can be used to change our reality.

If you are looking to have a love partner in your life, you must (1) be who you are, (2) assess who you are, and (3) realize what you value in your life. Sorry, but if you are serious about trying to find a quality partner with whom you are compatible, there is just no getting around these first steps.

Once we have taken time out to discover who we are and what we value, we are then able to make decisions in our life that are congruent with this knowledge of Self. A congruent life is one in which our outside behavior and circumstances reflect the inner Self. Being aware of who we are and making decisions in accordance with this awareness helps us to create a world around us that allows us to implement who we were created to be. Unless you really take a good hard look at yourself, you will not be ready to effectively find a fulfilling relationship.

Love is for the Courageous

Before you can even start your search for a love partner, you have to ask yourself if you are ready. Relationship shopping is not for the weak of heart. It is only for people who have enough courage to risk heartbreak. Like so many other things in life worth having, there is often risk involved.

If you want to make beautiful music with a love partner, then you have to have the courage to open your heart and life to another human being. This requires vulnerability. Many people are afraid of losing themselves. Are you ready for love? Love requires that you take off the armor around your heart and share your essence with someone else. This can be too intimidating for some.

It was too intimidating for Jenny. She was very attractive and had no problem finding a boyfriend. In fact, she usually went from one boyfriend to another. It was her pattern to flirt with a young man. Then, as the love would grow between the couple, Jenny's anxiety would grow even faster. The more the love grew, the more Jenny withdrew. Consequently, each relationship eventually ended.

When asked about this pattern, Jenny revealed that she was really scared of the relationship ending and that she did not want to be vulnerable enough to be hurt whenever it did end. Therefore, she guarded her heart. She would be very loving and affectionate with her boyfriends until love and intimacy began to take form. Then a subconscious alarm would go off. That's when she would launch conscious sabotage on the relationship. Jenny would self-fulfill her own prophecy of an ended relationship, the very thing that she was guarding against. Each ended relationship would confirm her belief in not trusting people and justify her pattern of withdrawing. I am happy to report that Jenny eventually received help. These days she is happily married with children.

We can psychoanalytically theorize about object relations and why people may be afraid to love. However, I think it's more effective to work with people's cognitive paradigms. This is what I did with Barry. Barry was lonely, and deeply wanted a significant other. Similar to Jenny, each time he found someone, he withdrew and eventually sabotaged the relationship. However, Barry went about the sabotage in his own special way. He wanted a guarantee that the relationship would not end and that he would not have to experience the pain of rejection. If he could not extract a guarantee, he wanted me to give some advice that would help him to behave in such a way that would ensure a perpetual relationship with his partner. In Barry's mind, a relationship was not successful if it ended.

During counseling I was able to help Barry see that, all relationships come to an end, either through a breakup or death. I told him that the point of a love relationship was not making it last forever but rather enjoying the journey. I used a metaphor of a ride at an amusement park. You get on the ride, and you have a great time, enjoying it as long as it lasts. But, guess what? It ends. There is nothing we can do that will change this reality. Therefore, if we want the joy and fulfillment of a love relationship, we need to accept this reality and gather enough courage to participate in the ups and downs of the ride called love. Barry finally found the courage to accept this reality, and accepting it has changed his love life for the better.

If you are afraid of the loss of love and, therefore, are also afraid of love itself, you really need to accept the temporary nature of all things in life and find the courage to still participate. Barry finally learned a great truth that is simply stated in Olive Ann Burns' novel *Cold Sassy Tree*. One of the characters says that life is like pouring water into a Coca-Cola bottle. If you're scared, you can't do it.

So, if all this is too scary for you, and you don't think you can do it, then put this book down. You are wasting your time reading it and are not ready for a love relationship. But, don't throw the book away! Just put it back on the shelf. The great thing about books is that you can always come back to them. When you get tired of superficial relationships and feel ready to harmonize with another soul, dust off this book and read some more. For those of you who already have the courage to love, we've got some work to do in order for you to find that love partner. So, keep reading, and let's get busy.

Primary Exercises

I believe you will find it helpful to take time out and complete the following exercises. In the first one, write any answers that you feel are pertinent to the self-exploration questions. You do not have to answer all of the following suggested questions. However, the more you answer, the better understanding you may have of yourself.

The following questions are just suggested primers to get you started on your reflective journey. You may think of some others that are worth exploring, as well. However, start with those below and be honest with yourself, when listing both strengths and weaknesses. The more honest you are in this whole process, the more you will get out of it.

The Harmonious Way *SELF DISCOVERY EXERCISES*	
1. What am I like physically?	
A. Am I tall or short?	
B. Am I over-weight or too skinny?	
C. Is my face attractive or plain?	
D. Is my body in good shape or in need of exercise?	
E. What is my most attractive feature?	
F. What is my least attractive feature?	
G. Do I want to change how I look for myself, rather than to please someone else?	

NOTES

2. *What am I like spiritually?*

A. What religion do I believe in?

B. What denomination is that religion?

C. Am I non-denominational?

D. Am I universal and accepting of many

different types of religious beliefs?

E. What is my theology ?

F. What are my philosophies about life,

politics, etc.?

<u>NOTES</u>

The Harmonious Way *SELF DISCOVERY EXERCISES*	
3. What am I like emotionally?	
A. Do I have a hard time expressing my feelings?	
B. Do I have a difficult time with some emotions more than others do?	
C. Am I very emotional?	
D. Am I a romantic?	

<u>NOTES</u>

4. *How do I relate to and communicate with other people?*	
A. Am I friendly?	
B. Am I non-assertive, assertive or aggressive?	
C. Do I act like a parent, an adult, or a child when I am around certain types of people?	
D. Do I like socializing with a lot of different people or just a few people?	
E. What is my sense of humor like?	
F. Am I open and honest?	
H. Am I pretentious ?	
I. Do I prefer face-to-face, telephone, or written communication?	
J. Am I verbose or brief and straight to the point?	
K. Do I listen to others?	

NOTES

The Harmonious Way *SELF DISCOVERY EXERCISES*	
5. What are my interests?	
A. What types of music do I like?	
B. What types of sports do I enjoy	
playing or watching?	
C. What types of movies or television programs do I like?	
D. What types of magazines and books do I like?	
E. What subject matters interest me?	

<u>NOTES</u>

The Harmonious Way *SELF DISCOVERY EXERCISES*	
6. What am I like financially?	
A. What are my assets?	
B. What are my liabilities?	
C. What is my net worth?	
D. What is my attitude toward saving and investing?	
E. What is my attitude toward debt?	

NOTES

The Harmonious Way *SELF DISCOVERY EXERCISES*	
A. What are my financial goals?	
B. What are my physical goals?	
C. What are my relationship goals?	
D. What are my family goals?	
C. What do I want to do before I die?	

<u>NOTES</u>

The Harmonious Way *SELF DISCOVERY EXERCISES*

A. What is most important to me in life?
B. What are my priorities?
C. What would make me miserable if I couldn't have it?
D. Is my family or career more important?

NOTES

The Harmonious Way *SELF DISCOVERY EXERCISES*
9. What type of personality do I have?
A. Am I mostly extroverted or introverted?
B. Am I mostly intuitive or sensing?
C. Am I mostly thinking or feeling?
D. Am I mostly judging or perceiving?

NOTES

The Harmonious Way *SELF DISCOVERY EXERCISES*
10. How do I like to spend my leisure time?
Dancing?
Watching TV?
Going to movies?
Going out with friends?
Drinking?
Clubbing?
Traveling?
Just talking?
Reading?
Walking?
Making love? (Etc.)

NOTES

All of these questions may seem overwhelming at first. Don't let them intimidate you into skipping this whole step. Just don't worry about it and do the best you can. I wrote this book to help you, not burden you. I do encourage you to give it a try. Not only is it the most important and primary step, you may be surprised to find you enjoy the process. And, it does lead you toward a goal you want to reach.

If you really get into this process and find yourself enjoying the self-exploration, you may want to consider seeing a counselor to help you explore some of these issues more fully. Many people are under the mistaken impression that counselors are only for "crazy" people. This is far from true. Many counselors see people for normal concerns and personal growth issues. As a matter of fact, some counselors prefer to see only people with these types of concerns.

Must I Change Who I Am?

Let's say that you are free from an unfulfilling relationship or have never even been in a relationship. How do you go about choosing a new partner?

Some will recommend that you change who you are. "You need to learn more about sports." "You need to start watching romantic movies and soap operas." "Whatever the object of your affection likes, you need to like the same thing." "If he is Republican, then you need to become Republican." "If she likes alternative music, then you need to learn to like it." "If he is Muslim, then you need to convert." In other words, if you want someone to like you, then you need to change who you are and become more like that special someone.

Don't believe such hype. The problem with that type of philosophy is, if you follow it, you are not being true to your Self. There is nothing wrong with making changes in your life. However, when the changes are made just to please others and not ourselves, then we are turning our back on who we really are. We are cutting against the grain of who we were created to be. We say to the devil, "Make that person love me, and I will give you my soul in return."

Earlier, I mentioned having a college friend who believed that you had to be dishonest if you wanted to find a loved one. Even though I considered this philosophy at different times in my life, I knew deep down that this was not the path for me. If I was looking for someone to spend the rest of my life with, I knew I had to be able to be me. More and more I learn that anything less creates a living hell.

What's love got to do with it?

Tina Turner

Chapter 5

What Type Person Do I Want My Partner to Be?

After you have begun the on-going process of discovering, admitting, and accepting who you are, start creating a picture of your ideal partner. When considering this, it may be helpful to recall the information from the first exercise. Here's why. Most happy people are able to implement their self-concept. In other words, they can be who they were created to be. In my personal life, as well as my professional one, I've found that many of us are in a tug-of-war between doing what we want to do and doing what other people want us to do. You may notice this, too; notice it in practically all aspects of your life. Relationships are no exception.

When you become involved with a partner, both of you will have conscious and unconscious needs and a sizeable list of expectations of the other. There is nothing wrong with this; it's just the way of nature. You will also want to continue being who you are, and your partner will have the same feelings about himself or herself. The result of the pull and push of these two dynamics can be a great deal of tension, if what each of you wants proves to be in opposition to the other.

For example, if you feel a need for frequent sex; however, your partner needs little or none, there it is: tension. And, a lot of tension, at that. Nobody is right; nobody is wrong. The two of you are just incompatible in that arena. Unless you want a miserable life, the best partner for you is one who allows you to be you, and meets your relationship needs. What type of partner can do this for you? A compatible one. Compatible partners are people with whom you have a great deal in common. If you can find someone who has the same needs, values, interests and personality as you, then you have found someone with whom you can travel through life. Both you and your partner will be who you were created to be, and your commonality will avoid unnecessary tension.

No two people are exactly alike. But the more alike you and your partner truly are when you first meet, the better. Not only will you have companionship, you will also have someone who can understand your world, allow you to be you, and give you what you need. You can do the same, in return.

You may have heard couples who have been together for some years express disappointment over the fact that they have grown apart. They still love one another, have no desire to part company, and still have many things in common. However, earlier, they shared a greater number of interests and desires. As the years passed, their interests began leading them in different directions. She got tired of golf and discovered she has a talent for bridge. He now finds bridge tiresome, while golf has become his avocation. They used to enjoy dancing, but his taste in music got stuck in the era when they were in school, while her taste welcomes the newest and latest in sounds and rhythms. Although there are many things couples such as these can do to renew their closeness, the point that needs making here is the more compatible you are when your relationship begins, the less the impact of any changes you experience that are not in lock step with one another.

An incompatible partner may accompany you through life and sometimes give you what you need. Often he or she will do this out of obligation, duty, and some resentment. I think it is safe to say that most of us are like God, in that we also love "cheerful" givers. Any other types of gifts are appreciated... but sometimes not quite as satisfying. Think about it. In the bedroom, would you prefer a sacrificial lover to give you what you want

66

with a perfunctory attitude? Or would you want a selfish lover who passionately enjoys pleasing you and himself or herself when making love to you? Personally, I prefer the latter.

Creating a Mate

Now comes the fun part. This is the point where we create our ideal mate. The following charts are exercise guides to help you define the mate whom you would most prefer. These charts can help you identify and attract a harmonious life partner. You start by listing the characteristics that you want your ideal mate to have. Don't just list physical characteristics. If you need ideas, look at Primary Exercises in the previous chapter to help get your creative juices flowing. Break out a couple of sheets of clean paper, or start yourself a relationship notebook or file where you keep these exercises and other notes about your relationship endeavors. Make what I call "My Dream Partner's Characteristic List." Enumerate as many characteristics as you feel you need in order to paint a definitive portrait of the ideal. After doing this, I had listed 42.

At a workshop I was leading, one of the participants asked me, "On my list, is it wrong to discriminate against guys I just don't find attractive?" I told her that when it comes to love relationships, discrimination is a good thing. To discriminate is to be able to carefully observe distinctions. This is necessary and good if you want to find a compatible love partner. Discrimination is wrong if we use our observations to treat a group of people unjustly. An example is if one discriminates in matters such as civil rights. And, this is the context in which most of us are familiar with the word. That type of discrimination is not the context we arc concerned about in this book. We are concerned about finding you a compatible partner with whom you can live a harmonious existence. This requires good judgment on your part. In order to assure yourself good judgment, you must become consciously aware of the difference between what you want and what you don't want in a love partner. When you meet potential love partners, you should discriminate between those who fit your needs and those who don't. When you develop the knowledge base and courage to discriminate, you may find yourself discriminating against someone your friends or family consider the catch of the century.

So have fun with your list. Include only what you truly want - not what you think you should have. If you like men who have a certain financial status, put it down. If you like women who look a certain way, write it down. This is your list, and you do not have to justify it to anyone. List as many characteristics as you like. And, remember: my list contained 42 characteristics.

The Harmonious Way *SELF DISCOVERY EXERCISES*
My Dream Partner's Characteristic List
1.
2.
3.
4.
5.
6.
7.
8.
9.
10.
11.

In the movie *Weird Science*, two young men entered characteristics of their perfect woman into a computer. A few moments later, the computer produced their perfect woman, live and in the flesh. Unfortunately, our technology hasn't reached that point. Until it does, you can use The Harmonious Way to find your ideal mate.

When I became of age, my mother took be to her side.
She said, "Son, you're growing up now,
*   pretty soon you'll take a bride."*
And, then she said, "Just because you've become
*   a young man now,*
There 're still some things that you don't understand now.
A pretty face come a dime a dozen.
Better find one that's going to get you true lovin',"
My momma told me, "You better shop around!"

Smokey Robinson

Chapter 6

How Do I Find a Love Partner

So how do you go about finding your ideal love partner? That is our question, now that we have all the tools and information we need. This chapter gives you practical information and guidance that can aid you in your hunt for a love relationship. But, before we do that, I must ask the following question for those who are already involved in a love relationship.

Should I Leave My Present Partner?

"Am I with the right person?" This is a question that many of you have probably asked yourself. And, these are other familiar questions: "Am I going to be able to make this relationship work, or should I leave?" "What if I can't find anyone else?"

The Harmonious Way is not about love conquers all. Staying in a relationship that is without harmony, for the sake of "love," can lead to much unhappiness for both partners. Whatever the cause of this type of over-commitment, be it stubbornness or a proud refusal to admit that you made a mistake, the end result usually does not feel very loving for either of the parties involved.

Love may be able to conquer all. The real question is *How long are you willing to suffer to find out?* I've seen people brush that question aside with comments such as, "If we love each other, that's all that counts. We should be able to handle anything in our relationship."

Loving or liking each other is good, of course, and these types of comments make good sound bytes. But when it comes right down to the day-to-day living with each other, you need a fair degree of compatibility in your relationship. The Harmonious Way promotes compatibility as one of - if not the most, important of the factors involved in having a successful happy long-term love relationship.

Before you get married, I could ask you and your partner if you love each other? On the other hand, if I am genuinely concerned about the success of your relationship, I could ask: "Can you live with each other?"

Zack and Charlene's story is one about being willing to suffer and do without love in the name of "love." There was a time when they were madly in love with each other. Charlene was very charming and beautiful; Zack was the attractive, quiet academic type. Charlene became pregnant; so, they married. After their daughter was born, Charlene gradually changed. She emotionally shut down and began withdrawing more and more from Zack and his family. She and Zack had two more kids, and Charlene became more and more distant from her family, as well. She also became fatter and fatter, as their situation worsened. To list the highlights, she started not coming home at night and hanging out with the wrong crowd, would never hold a steady job, and was in and out of trouble with the law. Zack even caught her with another man. For over 25 years Zack and Charlene endured a stressful, chaotic, tumultuous life together.

When Zack came to see me and shared his story, their youngest son had just graduated from high school and entered college. Zack had left home, too. He moved in with his brother because he was tired of being mistreated and feeling lonely all those years. "Now that our kids are all grown," Zack told me, "I finally feel free to leave, and that's exactly what I'm going to do."

I talked to him about establishing a counseling relationship, but after our time together I didn't hear from him. A couple of months later, I followed up with him to find out what was going on, and he reluctantly admitted that he and Charlene were back together. When I asked him if things had changed, he said that they had not. "I just couldn't bear to be without her. I love her so much, and that's what really counts, doesn't it?"

I felt sorry for Zack, but I also recognized that even though Charlene had mistreated him for many years, he must remain with her for some reason. He must be getting rewarded in some way. I don't know what psychological factors continue to keep him in his dysfunctional relationship. Maybe these factors would have been revealed with further counseling. Whatever the causes, Zack was not ready to leave his relationship, no matter how bad it was. What is even sadder is, in cases like Zack's and Charlene's, if the abusive partner recognizes the other party's dependency on him or her, the abusive behavior usually increases.

Zack was addicted to Charlene. And just like other addictions, even though they are bad for you, the pleasure they provide or the need they fill can overwhelm rational thought and behavior. Being addicted to a person can be just as damaging to our lives as addiction to drugs, when the addiction keeps us in dysfunctional situations.

Zack was not able to leave his situation, and he was willing to forego having harmony in his life. But, you do not have to continue in a relationship that is providing nothing other than stress and disharmony for you and for your partner. Many people are in relationships that are unfulfilling. Either their partners have changed or their personal needs and values have changed. If that's *your* situation, should you stay in the relationship or should you leave?

There are many reasons we can come up with that tell us why we shouldn't leave a relationship. "Divorce is wrong." "I don't want to hurt his feelings." "What about the kids?"

Numerous people get married for some very weak reasons. "She's so fine!" or "Boyfriend is getting paid!" These are the declarations that precede many marriages that are entered into by people who later discover that it takes more than things, such as physical attractiveness or material wealth, to make a relationship work. But often this discovery comes late, after a commitment has been made, after it becomes clear they are living with just a roommate, not a soul mate.

A Desert Tale

Imagine you are driving from Las Vegas to Los Angeles. You see a man not that far off the road in the middle of the desert, and there's no automobile in site, except yours. Thinking something may be wrong, you pull over to see if you can offer some assistance. When you get out of your car and began walking towards him, you notice that this distraught man is digging a hole in the ground.

"Excuse me, sir," you say to him, "is everything all right?"

Drenched in sweat, and sounding as if he is about to cry, he replies, "Oh, I'm fine, I'm just very thirsty; so, I'm digging a well."

You offer to take him to the nearest service station, but he refuses your offer. "No, that's okay, I'll just keep digging until I hit water."

You politely ask him if he thought he could find water in this desert? And, he says, "If I just dig a little bit longer, a little deeper, I'm sure this dry land will give me what I'm digging for."

It's too hot standing out in the desert to continue the discussion; so, you get into your car and drive down the road. When you get to a service station, you buy an ice-cold bottle of water, open it, and enjoy the cool thirst-quenching wetness, as it flowed down your throat. Then you stop and think about the man in the desert and wonder: Why did he put off enjoying this wonderful, refreshing gift from God?"

This is a sad but accurate metaphor for the way people often go about pursuing love relationships. They choose the desert (a person they want to be their partner) and dig for water (the love they so desperately need).

Many of us will try to love others into changing, only to rediscover, again and again, that he or she doesn't change, and we are not loved in return. When we try and try to bring about changes that only we want, we are like the man in the desert, trying to get water out of dry and barren land. "I'll just love her a little bit more; she'll come around."

I ask people, such as this, "Why don't you look somewhere else?" Invariably they reply, "No, that's okay, I'll just keep loving until I get loved in return."

And it continues, year after year. All the while, they are missing out on the wonderful gift of love that life has to offer them, ignoring the fact that there are many people who are ready to love them right now. If you are one of these "love well diggers," let me ask you: *How long do you want to go on in life without experiencing a truly wonderful love relationship? How long are you going to dig for water in a desert?*

Some of us know that the relationships we are in aren't right, but we don't have enough courage to break them off. Perhaps that was Charlene's situation. As Gladys Knight used to sing, "Neither one of us wants to be the first to say goodbye." We do care about the person; still we want to break up because, deep down, we know that it isn't going to work. And to top things off, our unwanted partner is so nice, that to break up with him or her would make us feel like heels. So, out of cowardice, we put up with the relationship and begin to cheat on the very person we are trying to protect from heartache.

If we really cared about the person whom we no longer want to be with, maybe the better alternative would be to call off the relationship, which would not only free ourselves, it would also free the other person. Then, instead of having one soul feeling trapped in a relationship and another soul feeling unloved, the world can have two liberated souls that are free to find the love they both deserve. Just as courage is required to enter a love relationship, it is also required to end one.

When Kent became my client, he was feeling stuck in his relationship with Rose. He didn't have the courage to leave her because Rose was blameless. She gave Kent everything and was very loving. However, Kent knew that he was not in love with Rose and had no intention of having a permanent and committed relationship with her, which was what she desperately wanted.

Kent let things drag on, without communicating how he felt; consequently his resentment toward Rose grew. His grades began to suffer, and he was usually miserable throughout the week. At meetings of the session group he attended, Kent spent a great deal of time, griping about his situation at home. When I asked him why didn't he end the relationship, Kent said that he gives Rose clues, but she doesn't pick up on them. I told him that was because Rose did not want to pick up on them. So, we worked on Kent's lack of courage to communicate directly and assertively with others, rather than through hinting games.

People deserve to know where they stand with each other. Otherwise, there is game playing, and someone is usually being hurt through the deception that arises out of fear of hurting her or his feelings. The truth was that Kent cared for Rose as a person but not as a love partner.

Though he cared about her, Kent did not have enough courage to communicate how he felt. This manifested in his withdrawing from the relationship and Rose being confused by Kent's behavior and feeling she was unloved. The more unloved she felt, the harder she tried to win Kent's affection. She was convinced that the fun and romance they had when they began dating was still possible in their future. Kent wasn't. But, in his mind, leaving Rose meant having to be the villain, a self-perception he could not accept. So, he subconsciously made Rose the villain, blowing up at her over little things, continuously finding fault.

In counseling, Kent recognized that no one had to be the villain for a relationship to end. He was able to recognize that both of them were good people; however; they just were not compatible. So, during one of our sessions, Kent practiced breaking-up-with-Rose scenarios. During the practice, Kent did his best to phrase his words so that Rose's feelings would not be hurt. He said things like, "I *think* I need some time to myself *right* now." "We can still be friends." or "We can still go out sometimes."

Phrases such as these come from people who are trying to soften the blow of the break up. The phrases are well intentioned, but they really do a disservice to the person being dumped. Here's why: they provide the dumpee with false hope while the dumper knows there is no hope for the relationship.

After a couple of practice sessions, Kent was able to break up with Rose firmly and respectfully. Rose was hurt, but at least she was not being dragged on with false hope. Both of them were then able to pick up the pieces and get on with their lives.

Kent told me he felt much happier since his definitive break up. He also said he had a lot more energy and was able to concentrate better on schoolwork. Rose was still trying to maintain a relationship with him, but it was much clearer now where they stood with each other.

If you do decide to break up with your current partner, then you must find the courage to make the break a clean one. Any new potential partner doesn't deserve to be caught up in drama or unfinished business that you have with an old love partner. It's a big world with a lot of people in it. You and your former partner do not have to stay in touch or try to maintain a friendship in order to absolve guilt from a break up. The sooner you and your "ex" can achieve a clean break, the closer both of you will be to finding new, compatible love partners.

A love relationship needs to have only two people involved in its development. Old boyfriends and girlfriends just complicate matters and may sabotage a potentially wonderful love relationship before it even gets off the ground. So, do yourself and any new love partner a favor; resolve any unfinished business you have with former love partners before trying to develop a new relationship. Here's a hint: if you find yourself explaining to a potential partner that you and your "ex" are "just friends," then more than likely you still have some unfinished business.

Incompatibility, such as in Kent's and Rose's case, is not the same thing as a decline in passion. Don't give up a good thing for something new and freshly thrilling. The newness of all relationships eventually wears off. In psychology, we know that repeated exposure to any stimulus weakens the response. Romance, passion, and excitement are the products of newness in a relationship. If you make the mistake that many people do and equate these things with love, you will find yourself bouncing from one relationship to another.

By following *The Harmonious Way*, you can move beyond hit-or-miss relationships to more productive ground. Your mate selection, when you follow *The Harmonious Way*, is based on compatibility, not on fickle emotions that will eventually fade. So, if you are comfortable with your present partner, yet your relationship works, don't overreact to the doldrums. Instead, go ahead and read the chapter on Love Maintenance. Also, sit down with your partner and talk about ways you can spice up your love life with each other. Then do it! If you end a good relationship for something you think will be better, you will probably regret it.

Another client of mine, Natalie, has lived the life of a romance novel heroine. She and Joe were both from a small Georgia town. They were very much in love and were considered an ideal couple. The two of them had been together for a couple of years in high school and had grown to be very comfortable with one another. But, graduation from high school brought complications into their relationship. Following graduation, Natalie was fortunate enough to be able to go to Los Angeles to join a theater group for the summer. When she returned in the fall, Joe noticed that Natalie was acting differently. What he did not know was that she had met Robert while she was in Los Angeles, a worldly, "cool" sort of guy whom Natalie found simply intoxicating. Robert showed Natalie a great time while she was in California, and she adored the excitement of it all.

That winter, after returning home, Natalie got called to the Coast for a small part in a production. Off she flew to Los Angeles, once again, leaving Joe behind. In April, Natalie announced to her family and friends that she and Robert would be getting married in June. And that's what happened. Following a nice church wedding in Georgia and their honeymoon, she moved into Robert's West Coast apartment.

Technically, Natalie and Robert had known each other for a year, but actually this year consisted of only a few months together in the same location. Two months after the big wedding day, I began a counseling relationship with Natalie. She was separated from her husband and had come home to Georgia to regroup and get herself together.

During the process of sharing her story with me, Natalie began to recognize the mistakes she had made. She saw that she had been swept away by brief romantic interludes with her long distance boyfriend. When she and Robert were finally together, the real Robert began to show his face. He was no longer focused on her and often stayed out all night. When he was home, he barely spoke to her, preferring to work on his car. When they did have time together, they had nothing to talk about. It wasn't long before they went from being passionate lovers to nothing more than two people who shared living space.

I began explaining *The Harmonious Way* to Natalie, believing it could help her find the right love partner, to understand what she needed in a relationship in order to find happiness. The exercises involved in employing my self-discovery techniques helped her to recognize that she and Robert were not in a harmonious relationship. She began to despair, seeing no hope in their future together. I was able to convince her that she could still find the love she was looking for in life - even if it wasn't with Robert. Fortunately, she and Robert did not have any children; therefore, this allowed Natalie even more freedom to make a clean break from him. Still, she really didn't want to divorce Robert because she was embarrassed by the fact that their marriage hadn't worked out.

I asked her to list, on a *Potential Partner Chart*, other men whom she knew. When she did, you can probably guess who scored highest. Yes, Joe led the pack by a mile. Even though she had listed Joe as a potential partner, she was very much afraid of trying to reestablish a relationship with him after she had "dissed" him, the way she had.

I told her that often pride keeps us from going after the things we know we need in our lives. But, in order to stop doing without a fulfilling relationship, we have to learn to swallow our pride and admit that we are only human. Moreover, because we are human, we make mistakes and will continue to make mistakes. I told her that, only after she accepted her mistakes, would she be able to divorce Robert and rebuilt her relationship with Joe. So, Natalie returned to LA, convinced of what she had to do.

Two years later, I was at a concert in a park with my family and heard someone call my name. It was Natalie. She came up to me and introduced herself; however, I remembered and recognized her, even though she looked different. Number one, she was smiling, and number two, she was pregnant. We caught up a little bit, talked about her pregnancy, and she introduced her husband to me. "Dr. Turpeau, I want you to meet my husband, Joe."

Back to the question: Is it the right time to find a new partner? If you are in a fulfilling relationship, then the answer to this question is "No." Don't fall victim to "the grass is greener on the other side of the fence" type of thinking. Sometimes it's greener because it has more manure.

Enjoy and celebrate your partner and consider yourself blessed. However, if you are not in a fulfilling relationship and you have done everything that you can do to try to make the relationship you are in work, then let me ask you this question: *Is it the right time to love and be loved?* Answering this question will also give you the answer to the first question in this paragraph.

If you and your partner have children, I hope you try counseling and everything else, before you decide to go separate ways. Don't deprive your children of parental love because you and your partner are not compatible. Asserting your right to be loved does not free you from your responsibility to be a parent. Children deserve love and discipline from both of their parents. Even if it means more arguing with your partner, do your best to communicate love to your children. Carrying their picture around in your wallet and saying, "I love my kids," just isn't enough.

Let the Shopping Begin!

So, now you are ready to begin your exciting search for a love partner. Remember that the goal is to find someone who has as many characteristics on your *Dream Partner's Characteristics Chart* as possible. You are more than likely not going to find someone who has all of the dozens of characteristics on the list, but the more the better. Here is a chart you might want to keep as you meet people you think could be potential partners.

Put a check beside each characteristic that your potential partner has. Draw your own chart to make room for more characteristics and potential partners.

The Harmonious Way POTENTIAL PARTNER CHART			
Characteristic	Person A	Person B	Person C
1.			
2.			
3.			
4.			
5.			
6.			
7.			
8.			
9.			
10.			

Everyday before you go out, look at the Characteristic List you've made. Then when you return home in the evening, break out the *Potential Partner Chart* and start working with it. Make sure you use pencil when filling out both exercises because the data will more than likely change the more you get to know your potential partners. You may also find yourself spotting characteristics in one of the prospects that you want to add to your *Dream Partner's Characteristic List.*

Avoid Going After Only One or Two Characteristics

During most of my dating career, I made the mistake of having only one characteristic requirement for a potential partner. My potential partner had to be what I considered to be physically attractive. Now you may be thinking this is a very superficial characteristic for someone to have, and I agree. Even though you are right, it was an important value to me. The mistake was not in the value itself, but in my having only one characteristic requirement.

The pitfalls of having a very short list remind me of Darlene, who is married to a professional football player. She was attracted to her husband because he was rich and famous. He was attracted to her because she was physically attractive. The two are still married and now have children, but Darlene is very unhappy. She and her husband are not friends. They have very little in common and constantly argue to the point that he has a history of being physically abusive to her. They are both victims of focusing on just one or two characteristics, rather than carefully choosing more compatible mates.

You cannot build a long lasting relationship if your partner has only one characteristic that you value. Each person has different values and preferences. It is not for anyone else to judge whether or not your values and preferences are valid. Let others talk if they must. Remember: you are going to be the one spending a great deal of time with your future partner; therefore, that time might as well be with someone that you value and appreciate.

Don't Get Hung Up Over One Characteristic

If a certain characteristic is not that important to your being able to live happily with a person, then don't get hung up on it, if everything else is right. Sally, a client of mine, is a textbook case of this mistake. Sally was a very productive, genuine, attractive, and ambitious student. Other young women looked to her as a role model because her life seemed a non-stop series of successes. Sally graduated with honors from college, had a masters degree, and was involved in some entrepreneurial endeavors. Sounds like the making of a perfect life. But Sally had a problem and came to me for advice. "Why can't I find Mr. Right?"

She had experienced a couple of serious relationships, but neither of them lasted. For the past couple of years she had been looking for someone but was unproductive in her search. This was especially frustrating for Sally, who was used to achieving her goals. It didn't help matters that many of her close friends were now getting married.

We spent some time talking about *The Harmonious Way* and the importance of finding a person with whom she was compatible. One day,

Sally mentioned that there was someone who scored very high on her *Dream Partners Characteristic List.* Surprised and excited for her, I asked her to tell her who he was? "His name is Stephen," she said. "But it wouldn't work between us because I'm a Christian and he's a Jew."

She went on to explain that Stephen was the brother of a friend of hers; moreover, she had stayed in close contact with Stephen since kindergarten. He and Sally had been the best of friends for years, and their families had even become friends with one another. She also said that there was a definite attraction between the two of them. So, I asked Sally if Stephen were Christian would she be dating him? Without needing a moment to consider the question, she said, "Definitely."

I told her that I thought it was a shame that the gift of love was staring her right in the face and that she refused to accept the gift from God because of ideological differences about the nature of Reality. I asked Sally what her denomination was? "Methodist," she said. I then asked her if she would have problems dating a Catholic? She said, "No." Furthermore, she agreed that the God of Christianity was also the God of Judaism. I then proceeded to show her that she could bridge differences in religious beliefs when dating. She had just arbitrarily drawn the line between Christianity and Judaism. I also said that the fact that she and Stephen were the best of friends was evidence that their differences in religious beliefs were not that big a hurdle for them.

Sally, conceded that they could get along, if they respected each other's religious viewpoints and practices. But, being the planner that she was, she was looking down the road to the time when the two of them might have children and the problem of deciding in which religious faith their offspring would be raised. I reiterated to her that would be something that she and Stephen would have to discuss and work on, based on each of their desires to raise their children within a particular religion. Sally and Stephen, I pointed out, had several options. If one partner feels that it is very important that the children be a certain religion and the other partner's preference for their children to be a different religion is not that strong, then there may be no conflict. The partner with the least firm stance could just voluntarily concede on this issue and let the kids be raised in the other's faith. Another option would be to expose the children to both religions and let them decide on their own, after they grow up. I told Sally that I had faith in her ability to work through these types of issues and felt confident about the future of their children.

She pursued a romantic relationship with Stephen, and he welcomed her expression of interest. She and Stephen are now in a committed relationship, and Sally says that the relationship has great potential. When we talk, it's easy to see that she is much happier now. Her old melancholy, solemn look has given way to a more joyful pleasant inner peace. And she is pleasantly surprised that the differences in their religious beliefs are not as big an issue as she thought they would be.

Virtual Relationships

The older I get, the less I appreciate television. When I was a boy, I couldn't get enough of the sitcoms, *Star Trek* episodes, and other adventure series. However, now that I'm older, time is much more at a premium and valued. Anything that wastes my time is the enemy. Television, the Internet, and video games are technological marvels. They are great and valuable in their own right; however, they can also easily become thieving bandits. Not only can they rob us of our time, they can take us away from rewarding human relationships.

We need to learn to get up from our chairs, get out, mingle and relate in person with others. Spending your time with fictitious characters on a television screen or interacting with video game personalities is artificial intimacy. Interacting with others over the Internet is, at least, a relationship with real people. However, hiding behind the safety of a computer screen can only take you so far in a relationship. A real love relationship must be in person.

That said, I need to add that Internet relationships can have value. They are good in that they allow us to get to connect with people and know whether or not we are compatible with them before we become distracted by their physical appearance. But, unless you don't plan to go beyond an electronic relationship, you really need to direct your energies toward establishing a relationship that is live and unplugged.

Don't Get a Pet

If you are alone, looking for a love partner, and considering getting a pet, don't do it. If you already have a pet, that's fine; however, if you do not, don't become a pet owner in the near future. Don't get me wrong. I love animals and have a pet dog named Sampson. The reason I advise you against owning a pet if you are looking for a love partner is because I want you to fully feel the pain of loneliness.

What?!

That's right, you read correctly; I want you to feel the pain of loneliness. Pet ownership can take the edge off loneliness. Other things that I've already mentioned, such as television and the Internet, as well as alcohol, drugs, or other obsessions can do this, as well. People often run to these things to avoid loneliness. But, one thing that is not apparent to many is the role pet ownership can play in preventing you from finding a love partner. While there are other distractions that perpetuate dull loneliness, pets are living creatures and, consequently, provide a measure of companionship. If you have no desire to have a human love partner, then there is no problem having a pet. But, if you truly want to have a human mate, then you need to feel the full effect of loneliness in order to be motivated to do something about your situation. If I begin to feel lonely and just curl up next to my dog or cat, the pain of loneliness will be reduced. At least Rover and Trixie love me. Right? The problem with this is a highly involved relationship with a pet can lull you into doing nothing to find a partner. This is the same problem with welfare programs.

Welfare programs are good, to an extent. The problem is that they satisfy the poor with monetary crumbs from the table of wealth. As long as you feed me with just the right amount of crumbs, I will never feel hungry enough to do something about my poverty. This is the same with pet ownership. It's good, but the intimacy is merely crumbs, when compared to the feast that can be shared with another human being. Many of us need to feel the pain of rock bottom in order to be motivated to change. Pet ownership buffers you from the full pain of loneliness that can actually motivate you to get up and out to fellowship with others. You can always get a pet later on. If you already have a pet, I'm not suggesting that you get rid of it. Just don't let the comfort of pet intimacy prevent you from experiencing human companionship.

If you think I'm being ridiculous and cold-hearted, that's fine. Tomorrow morning I'll more than likely wake up next to my wife's warm body, not the butt of a cat staring me in the face.

Exposure

What good is it for you to be the great and wonderful person that you are and with so much to offer, if nobody knows you exist? People need to interact with you. They need to know who you are. It pays to advertise.

If you are an introvert, there's nothing wrong with that. I certainly understand because I'm an introvert, too. However, if you want to find a love partner, you need to get over your introversion. At least temporarily.

I had a client who has a small build, wears glasses, and is very intelligent. Bill is from a little town in the Midwest. He complained about his new environment in the South; saying everyone seemed to be so superficial and talked about nothing. He gave this sweeping condemnation as his reason for avoiding parties, clubs, and social exposure of any kind. I suspect he had the same criticism of social events elsewhere. Bill was definitely an introvert and often said the things that I hear from other lonely introverts. "There isn't anybody out there for me, everybody else is so superficial. When I go to parties, I feel so out of place and unwanted. I'd rather stay home and watch television. Loneliness beats trying to fit in with people with whom I have nothing in common."

The problem is that introverts, such as Bill, do not realize that there are other introverts out there who have a lot in common with them. However, these introverts cut themselves off from exposure to one another. They pass the time pining away at home, feeling miserable and lonely. There is no telling how many times the Bills of this world were at a party or other gathering in which there was someone else a few feet away who was having the same thoughts of being lonely and disconnected. However, because of mutual introversion, insecurities, and prejudging everyone else as jerks, they never got to meet each other.

Am I describing you? If so, it's likely that the only people you get to meet are the social extraverts who do their best to have a conversation with you by talking about safe topics, such as the weather, sports or news in the headlines. So, their limited topics of conversation turn you off and make you feel even more alone and isolated than before you met these out-going, eager-to-please people we label extraverts.

I think Bill and the rest of you who find yourselves so turned off by superficial conversations need to ease up a little bit on other people. Human beings are very insecure creatures. Usually before they start spilling their guts to you about deep issues that really matter, they like to test the water by throwing out harmless topics to get a feel as to how you interact with others. Most of us don't like offending others, nor do we want to be hurt by others. So, our initial conversations take the form of a back and forth dance about routine matters such as the weather, sports, movies, or where you are from. People usually don't want to reveal their stance on abortion, gun control, or their relationship history in their very first conversation with you.

Here is my recommendation. The next time you find yourself at one of these events go ahead, accept, and play this conversation game. Maybe you won't be so frustrated by others. If you have the patience, you may find that you have come into contact with some very interesting people. Who knows? Possibly what starts as idle chitchat could turn into the love partnership of your life.

The main idea is for you to get out there and meet people. Join clubs and other organizations. Go to church. Go to parties. Go to nightclubs. All of these places are wonderful locations to meet potential partners.

Many people have a great prejudice against meeting potential partners in nightclubs. Most self-help books do not recommend them as likely spots for initiating a committed relationship. They tell you that, in a nightclub, the only type of person you will find is someone interested in a one-night stand. Bull!

Yes, there are people in the nightclubs looking for one-night stands. Yes, there are people in nightclubs who are afraid of commitment. But, there are many people in nightclubs who are looking for a long-term committed relationship. Again I say, ease up a little bit and don't be so quick to judge others harshly. There are many people in nightclubs who are lonely, looking for love, and are ready for an intimate relationship. These are people just like you.

Answer these questions.

- Have you ever been to a nightclub?
- Are you not a good person capable of loving and being in a long term intimate relationship?
- How realistic do you think you are being when you assume that you are the only one in the whole entire club who is worth knowing?

Dump the "holier than thou" role and go out to a club with some friends and have a good time. But, make sure you force yourself to meet new people. Oh, and by the way, I've been happily married to my wife, Michelle, since 1992. Can you guess where I met her? Here's a hint. It wasn't in church.

Be Assertive

You have a note that you were meant to play. If you are non-assertive, you are either not playing your note, or you are playing it too softly, muffling its appealing sound. You are not being heard and are cheating yourself out of the opportunity to express who you are. If you are at the other extreme, aggressive to the point that you play your note but do not allow others to play theirs, you are likely missing out on what others have to offer you. In order to have harmonious relationships, all notes need to be heard and resonate together. That is why it is imperative that all of you be assertive.

Let's make certain we understand what that word means. Assertion is often a misunderstood paradigm; so, let's see if we can clarify it. In the assertiveness model of human behavior there are three basic modes of behavior: Non-Assertion, Assertion, and Aggression.

* **Non-Assertion** is behavior characterized by allowing others to have their way at the expense of your desires.

* **Assertion** is attempting to gain your desires, while also allowing and respecting the desires of others to have their way.

* **Aggression** is going after your desires without any respect for or at the expense of the desires of others. On a behavioral continuum it would look something like this:

Non-Assertion------------**Assertion**--------------**Aggression**

In this model, Assertion is the ideal mode of behavior. More than likely, in different situations with different people, we find ourselves acting out of each of these modes; however, most of us have a tendency to operate out of one mode more than the others. We all fit somewhere on this continuum.

No doubt about it, some people are aggressive. They don't care about anyone else's needs but their own. You may have heard these people referred to as "bad boys" or "controlling women." Contrary to the belief of amateur psychologists, these people do not have low self-esteem. They have low other-esteem. They prey on people who are non-assertive - albeit unconsciously. The aggressive don't have much of a problem getting into a relationship. But, once they have a relationship, they tend to mistreat their partner; so, their relationship lasts only as long as the partner is willing to put up with the abuse. When the partner is finally fed up, he or she leaves, and the aggressor is left wondering what happened? Aggressors either don't see or minimize the problems in their relationships because they are getting their needs met. They think that the relationship is going well, which is not surprising given their insensitivity to the feelings and desires of others. Aggressors play their note so loudly that they drown out the other notes around them.

My mode of behavior for much of my early life was non-assertion. In my attempts to always be a nice boy, I would always put my needs below the needs of others. People would reward me and call me a good kid. But that wasn't enough because my needs often went unmet. This non-assertion spilled over into my dating behavior. At first, females were flattered, but it wouldn't take long before I started hearing: "You're too nice."

Despite hearing these words, I continued my search for someone who would appreciate the love I had to offer. Every time I inevitably heard the same words over and over again: "You're too nice."

Then one day, I ran across the assertiveness paradigm. My life was changed. Now the words, "You're too nice," made sense. Until then, I was morally arrogant and thought that everyone else didn't know what they were talking about. It finally dawned on me that people really don't respect non-assertive behavior, and that if you allow them to run over you, they usually will - while throwing you a reward crumb by calling you a nice boy.

My behavior changed from that point on. I still have non-assertive tendencies, but I worked hard at letting others know that I expect my needs to be met, as well. Gradually, I started noticing that I began having better success in my dating life. I also became a happier person overall. My light was shining: my note was being heard.

In counseling, I usually have more non-assertive clients than aggressive ones. This is probably because aggressors usually get their way, and when their relationships don't work out, it doesn't take them long to find someone else to take advantage of. As P.T. Barnum said, "There's a sucker born every minute." I usually find myself with the task of convincing my clients not to be that sucker.

This was the case with Pamela. Pamela was a client who had been referred to me by another therapist. She had been working with her previous therapist for almost two years, but both felt that not much progress had been made. Pamela presented a general melancholy and couldn't figure out why she wasn't happy in life. I learned that she was the oldest of her siblings and was the responsible one. She had spent her life caring for her family and friends. The more she talked, the more it seemed that Pamela was a walking doormat. She put her self at the beck and call of everyone in her life. Pamela didn't have any luck in the dating world either. At work, she constantly went out of her way to help her co-workers with their tasks, never receiving credit or thanks.

After diagnosing Pamela's problem as non-assertion, we began to work on building her assertiveness skills and changing her mindset. We worked on her mindset because people have to believe that they deserve to have their needs met. Otherwise, any behavioral change achieved would not be lasting. We talked about spirituality and her identity, as well as how the two relate. We talked about her expecting more from life and from other people. I gave her homework assignments that made her focus on her desires. We worked on affirmations, such as:

I am a good person.

I deserve to be happy.

I expect to have my needs met.

I am a child of God and expect to be treated as such.

My needs are just as important as other people's needs.

Behaviorally, I gave her homework assignments that required her to ask things *from* others. Believe it or not, as simple as this may sound, it was very difficult, at first, for Pamela to do these exercises. Her reaction was typical of the non-assertive. They tend to have a very strong desire to be a nice boy or a nice girl. They do not want to be aggressive, which they see as being mean to people. When I encourage people, such as Alicia, to engage in assertive behavior, their first response is usually resistance; they see their assertiveness as making them bad people. I'm usually able to convince them that they have a long way to go before they could possibly be considered aggressive. That is not their problem. Just as a four hundred-pound person has no imminent need to fear anorexia, non-assertive people have no need to fear being too aggressive.

After a while, Pamela began to realize that she deserved to have her needs met. Her behavior also began to change. She dressed up more. She began to say "no" to people more. I told her that she would begin to experience some tension with the people she normally related with because they were used to her being non-assertive. Just as predicted, she experienced some tension with others, but she held firm. She reported that she was being considered for a promotion at her job. She had not found a love partner by the time we ended counseling, but she did take the initiative to get out of a developing relationship. When asked Why?" she said that she believed she deserved better. Although, it would be nice to report that she had found the love of her life, our counseling relationship ended after three months because Alicia was happier and had the confidence that she could continue on her own.

My hope for you, as well as for Pamela, is that you will recognize the benefit of being assertive in your daily life. It has worked for me and for many of my clients. I am sure that it will help you find a love relationship in which you and your partner can express yourselves in harmony.

Be Attractive

Yes. You read correctly. Be attractive. No matter what God has given you to work with, it is up to you to make the most of it. Like it or not, when it comes to the dating game, physical attractiveness is important. Now some of my more lofty readers will say the point I'm making is superficial. They are the ones who will propound the virtues of being loved for who we are on the inside and that the outside appearance isn't important. Their virtuous perspective sounds good and gives us nice warm fuzzies on the inside, but unfortunately, it does not match reality. I agree with the view that the inside character of individuals is more important and that we would probably make much wiser mate selections if we were not distracted by physical appearances. But that is a very big IF.

In reality, physical appearance does exist, and it's a major factor in the relationship shopping game. If you insist on living according to the high ideal of "physical appearance doesn't matter" and you ignore its importance, then you will be greatly hindered in your search for a love partner. Whether we are conscious of it or not, all of our interpersonal relationships are influenced by the physical appearances of others. Our physical characteristics play a major role in how we treat and are treated by others.

I remember a woman named Nigeria. She was an A" student in college. If you looked really hard, you could see that she was also physically attractive. The problem was, you had to look really, really hard.

Nigeria was very lonely and wanted to have a boyfriend. But she never had any male callers. Her mother and others would recommend that she fix her self up. Unfortunately, Nigeria stubbornly held fast to her belief that her physical appearance did not matter; she wanted to find someone to love her for what is on the inside -- not the outside. The last time I saw her, Nigeria had graduated with honors from law school. She was far fatter than before and still refused to pay attention to her physical appearance. But, one thing hadn't changed; she was still lonely. And Nigeria was desperately in need of love.

Now, my critics may say that asking someone to fix himself or herself up is concentrating on the wrong thing and that I am asking people to change who they are. On the contrary, making an effort to look your best shows an appreciation of and respect for who you are. If you don't care about your physical appearance, then others won't care either. In the relationship shopping game, if people don't care how you look, then they don't care about you. Maybe this is a bad thing, but it is real. It takes courage on my part to be this honest because I know many readers will not like seeing anything that emphasizes the importance of something as superficial as physical appearance. However, I could not write a relationship book with integrity and leave this part out. Taking care of your physical appearance will carry you a lot further than ignoring how you look will. Requiring potential suitors not to care about your appearance is a very high standard that is difficult for them to comply with.

It is not impossible for you to find someone who does not care about your physical appearance. It just takes much, much longer. You will have to depend on natural, everyday interactions with others whom you casually meet and, even then, these new acquaintances may still not pay attention to you as a potential love partner. An attractive physical appearance is often a magnet that gets people's attention. The more attention you attract, the more people you will meet, and the greater the number of people who will eventually get to know the real you. But if you never get their attention because you refuse to play these superficial games, then only a few people will ever have the opportunity to get to know you as a potential love partner. The relationship shopping game is a numbers game; the more people you meet, the better. Don't let your high ideals about what *should be* form an obstacle that keeps you from meeting potential love partners. It's wiser, more practical, and more productive to recognize reality and live accordingly.

At one time in my career, I was a pastoral assistant. One of my responsibilities was the youth ministry of our church. Derek was one of the Rodney Dangerfield's of this group in their early teens. He didn't get any respect. Except for his Sunday bests, blue jeans, running shoes, tee shirts, and a pair of thick glasses with masking tape in the middle were the extent of his wardrobe, which was topped off by a bowl haircut. Derek would tell sick, dirty, unfunny jokes that only annoyed others. It was apparent that Derek did not care how he looked and that his jokes were a pathetic attempt for some type of attention.

One summer I noticed that Derek had not been coming to our youth group meetings for about two months. I asked around, but no one knew where he was, and they really didn't seem to care. Then, one Sunday evening that same summer, during our meeting, Derek walked through the door. Based on the reactions of the room, you would have thought the male equivalent of Cinderella was standing before us. Derek looked dramatically different. It was still Derek, but the packaging was more appealing. He was dressed in a casual dress shirt, nice pants, and perfectly shined dress shoes. He had a stylish haircut that made him seem more mature, and the geeky, patched glasses were gone. Derek was walking differently, as well. Rather than his usual goofy stride, he stood erect and moved with pride and confidence.

The reaction from the group was the only thing more remarkable than Derek's metamorphosis. As soon as he walked in, the females started to smile and whisper with one other. During the free times of the meeting, the young people came over to Derek to talk to him. This was a different experience for a young man who had always been the one trying to work his way into a group, only to be looked at with disdain and avoided. Now he, Derek, was the one being sought after. Now people were interested in getting to know him. I noticed that he wasn't acting silly and didn't try to crack his usual unfunny jokes. He didn't need to. People were attracted to him. From that meeting on, Derek was considered one of the leaders of the group, one of the members to whom the other youth looked up.

When I shared this story with my colleagues in one of my doctoral psychology classes, my colleagues were not pleased. I think it upset them that Derek had cooperated with the superficiality of reality. I think it would have pleased them more if Derek had been in counseling for years, being convinced that it did not matter what other people thought about him, learning that he should be happy with himself first, that he did not need to be externally validated. I understood their viewpoint. And, though my colleagues were not pleased, one thing remained true: despite their objections, Derek's life had changed for the better. He was now a happier and more fulfilled person.

Again, I agree that self-acceptance is very important, but the human organism is a social being. The affirmation we receive in our relationship with others is an important variable that must not be denied in our goal of self-fulfillment. To ignore or delay this area of our lives until we reach that elusive state of isolated self-happiness just won't cut it for most people. Relationships are a part of the cake of life, not the icing, as many would like for you to believe. We need relationship, and we need it now. *The Harmonious Way* asks you not to change who you are at your core. You need to be true to your inner Self, if you are to have a fulfilling life. Realistically, you need to change some behaviors and beliefs, if you want to change the results of your relationship shopping. Taking care of your physical appearance and making yourself more attractive is one of the behaviors that you may need to give more attention. It says that you respect who you are. If you do and show it, you will attract more people and give them the opportunity to discover the real inner you that may otherwise go unnoticed. Being attractive doesn't change who you are. It promotes who you are. Another P.T. Barnum quote comes to mind. "Without promotion, something terrible happens: NOTHING!" I'm sure Derek would agree.

Introducing Yourself

So, we have you armed with your *Dream Partner Characteristic List* and your *Potential Partner Chart*. You're getting exposure, and you're looking good. Then it happens. You see someone who attracts you. You are definitely interested in getting to know him or her. Your heart races with eagerness and excitement the closer you are to the person. You catch each other's eye, then you look away so as to appear that you are not staring. Time goes by. Eventually you work up enough courage to smile the next time your eyes meet. You receive a smile in return, and then a little while later, your potential partner leaves the room. Your eyes never to meet again. What happened?

What happened was the same thing that will always happen until you learn to face your fear of rejection and muster up enough courage to introduce yourself to strangers. Nothing. It doesn't matter if you are male or female; in today's society it is appropriate for either gender to introduce herself or himself to someone. Traditionally, men have had more experience introducing themselves to those they are interested in, but women are more and more realizing that they must have more control over their fates and not wait on men to decide with whom the women will interact.

We all fear rejection, to some degree. I've had my share of it in the past when I introduced myself to people I was interested in, only to discover that the interest was not mutual. It's not a good feeling to reveal your interest in someone and not have it reciprocated. Some of my earliest experiences with this pain of rejection occurred for me, as it did for many young boys, during house parties. Men, does this sound familiar? A slow song comes on the stereo, the lights dim, and girls go to one side of the room, boys to the other. You and the other boys confer with one another, regarding whom you are going to ask to dance. When the song is about halfway through, you finally gather enough courage to walk across the floor to ask the girl to dance. But, before you get there, someone else beats you to her. You resolve to move quicker next time, and as soon as the lights dim again, you are ready. As the genders take their places, you begin to take that long walk across the floor. All eyes are on you and trying to guess whom you are going to ask to dance. You finally reach the object of your affection and ask her if she'd like to dance? She replies with a simple "No." Your heart drops, your countenance falls, and you turn around to see your friends trying to hide their reactions to your rejection. "But, you keep your cool and play it off," as we used to say. Then you return to the male side of the room. But, this time the walk is even longer.

Let's face it, not everyone is going to like you or be interested in you the way you would prefer. That's a fact of life. Get used to it. Rejection can be a difficult pill to swallow, but we don't have to take it personally.

The Harmonious Way recognizes that it is an irrational belief to think that we can get along with everyone. *The Harmonious Way* respects diversity. If someone does not want to relate to you, then don't immediately throw a pity party for yourself. There are other people who will find you attractive or interesting. There are billions of people in the world with different tastes. You have something to offer to others who are interested in you. So, don't become obsessed with someone who does not return your affection. Move on. As the saying goes, "There are other fish in the sea." Meeting potential love partners is a numbers game. The more people you meet, the better. Therefore, you can't let potential partners get away without introducing yourself.

The ladies reading this should not tune out. As I said before, either sex can make the first move in today's world. So, ladies, if you see a man who appeals to you get a brush-off similar to the one just described, I assure you that you will never have a better opportunity of connecting with that guy. Move right in and say, "Hi, my name's, Lana, and I'd love to dance with you."

Even if the dance doesn't lead to romance, it will keep both of you from looking like wallflowers. Every guy in the room worth knowing will think you're one classy lady because of what you did and not be afraid to ask you for the next dance.

When I first started dating, I was slow to introduce myself. It finally dawned on me that, if I introduced myself to a female, one of two things would happen, and neither of them was something I couldn't handle. She could reject me, or she and I could start a conversation and possibly get to know each other better in the future. On the other hand, I could not introduce myself, which would assure that she and I would definitely not get to know each other and that there would be a continuation of my state of loneliness. Risking rejection creates the potential of winning at the dating game. Not risking keeps us in the category of loser" in the game of love.

I can hear some of you saying, "But I don't know what to say!" The answer is for you to just relax and be yourself. Sounds like a clichÈ, I know. But, it's really the best approach. Too many times people try to come up with creative, cute, funny ways and lines to introduce themselves, only to wind up ruining their introduction. People prefer introductory lines that are harmless or straightforward. So don't try too hard to be funny or creative. Just use statements such as: Would you like to dance?" ..."Excuse me, do you have the time?" ..."Hello, mind if I sit here?"..."So, where are you from?" All of these introductory lines and similar ones that you can probably think of are practical, everyday, non-offensive, and conversational. You'll be surprised how well they can work. From that point on, just continue to be yourself during conversation. If you still meet with rejection, you can at least be confident that it wasn't because you blew the opening line. And you can always tell yourself that it was the others person's loss. That always helps a little, as well.

Men and Women Are from Earth

Let's be real. As much as we like to have clear, specific instructions on how to relate to the opposite sex, life is not and never will be that simple. On Earth, yes, men and women may have some general tendencies, but in reality we are each a distinct individual who needs to be respected and treated as such. There is danger in trying to make blanket statements about men and women, such as Women are very emotional," or Men have problems with intimacy." The danger in accepting these statements is they provide a false sense of security, when dealing with others. On planet Earth, we are each a unique blend of characteristics. No two of us are precisely the same, and - here's the bad news - it's not likely that you will meet a person who fits all the gender descriptors that you have listed on your *Dream Partner Characteristics List.*

Out of a sense of frustration, we are often bewildered by our inability to have meaningful love relationships. We conclude that we just don't understand the opposite sex. So, when we discover a manual that claims to let us in on the secrets, we are tempted to believe that all men or all women fit the characteristics we just read about. Eventually, we discover that the person we are trying to relate to does not neatly fit the characteristics listed. To make matters even more confusing, the man you are interested in has some of the female characteristics, or the woman has some of the male characteristics. Back to the drawing board.

This same type of stereotypical thinking can lead people to give up on having a relationship with the opposite sex. Countless times I have heard clients and friends who have had a bad experience threaten to swear off trying to establish a romantic relationship. Then they go about sabotaging any new relationships because they expect the next potential partner to be just like the last. Some even avoid pursuing a love relationship all together.

The above scenarios speak to the need of respecting and treating potential partners and everyone else as individuals, rather than stereotyping them, based on gender. Human relations would be greatly improved if we would minimize the stereotypical thinking and take the time and expend the energy to get to know people on an individual basis. The key words are *time* and *energy*. In order to relate with someone effectively, you need to invest both time and energy into knowing him or her. We need to discover the person's likes and dislikes, what they value, and how they relate. There are no shortcuts.

The Harmonious Way recognizes that each individual is a unique note in the symphony of life. This symphony has more than a male note and a female note. There are as many notes as there are people. The more time you take to listen to each person's note, the more likely you are to know whether or not the two of you can harmonize.

To Have Sex or Not to Have Sex

In today's world, a single sexual interlude can mean a death sentence, if you have sex with someone who is infected with HIV. Though it may seem awkward at first, more and more people are requiring that their potential sexual partners be tested for the AIDS virus before intercourse takes place. It is not unreasonable for you to request this from your potential partner - or your partner to request it of you. If your potential partner has problems with the request, then run away fast. Anyone who cares about you and does not have anything to hide would not mind getting such a test. If he or she does, you are probably about to become involved with someone who doesn't care enough about you to protect you from harm.

And, what you ask of your partner, you should also be willing to do, as well. My suggestion is that the two of you go together for testing. Make it a mutual commitment and concern. It will turn what can seem a humiliating experience into a mutual bond that adds extra significance to any intimacy that may follow.

At what point do you get tested? The answer: when it seems as if the relationship is headed toward sexual intercourse, it's time. If you have been putting the subject off because you can't seem to find the right moment, let me give you a marker that will tell you when you have gone too far. If you and your partner haven't been tested and either of you has seen the other's body parts that a bikini barely covers, then "Warning…Warning!" you should have been tested by now. Stop fooling yourself. It's time to know whether either of you is a health risk for the other. When you and your partner reach this point, the two of you should make a date to go and take tests together, even if you have been tested before, even if you are a virgin. The AIDS virus can be acquired through means other than intercourse. Furthermore, it can go undetected for a long time, even after you have been infected; so, it can't hurt to be tested periodically. These facts also form a good reason to continue to use condoms for awhile, even if you and your partner test negative for the virus.

Time Together

Before walking down that aisle or jumping into the sack with a potential partner, it's wise to spend a great deal of time with this new person in your life. The two of you need to interact in many different situations. You need to see how the object of your affection behaves in different seasons throughout the year. How well is stress handled? What are his or her beliefs about having children? If you got a job somewhere else, would she or he be willing to move? Would you be willing to move for her or him? How does she interact with her family? How does he treat people? These questions are just a small sample of the ones that need to be answered when you are studying and learning about your potential partner.

While interacting with romantic prospects, I don't recommend giving them your *Potential Partner Chart* so that they can check off the characteristics they have. A much better method is your becoming a covert interviewer on your dates. Find out, through casual conversation, whether or not your potential partner has the characteristics that you are looking for. For example, during one encounter you could ask, What types of things do you like to do for fun?" Or say, "Tell me about your hobbies." Another encounter might provide the opportunity for you to ask about children or spiritual issues or another topic based on the situation or topic at hand. If you review your Characteristic List daily, you'll be able to remember to find out more information from your potential partner each time the opportunity arises. And, while you are collecting data, you might pass along some of your own. Let your interests be known. Volunteer the kind of information you hope the other party will share. That's a great way to get a two-way flow of information flowing.

The main thing is to spend enough time in different situations before you start believing that this person is "the one for me." You don't want to prejudge someone before you have had enough time to get to know one another. It takes time for the real person to come to light. The ideal self that people put forward early in the relationship can be deceiving. It's easy to put forward a too-good-to-be-true ideal self for a little while, but the real self eventually will have to show its colors. Warts and all. Then you have to decide whether or not you can live with those warts.

Waiting Too Long

I was abnormal among my peers in college because my primary concern, at the time, was looking for a mate. I had a steady girlfriend during the college years, but I laid the marital pressure on too thick, and not long after our engagement, she dropped me like a hot potato. After recuperating from this heartbreak, I got back to the business of looking for "Ms. Right." My tendency was to err on the side of jumping into a serious relationship too quickly.

Just as you can make a mistake by jumping into a serious relationship with someone too soon, you can also make a mistake by waiting too long to commit. And, more people make the mistake of waiting too long than the other way around. People wait too long to get into serious relationships for various reasons. Some think there is someone out there who is even a better match for them than their current partner, someone who meets all or at least virtually all of the characteristics on their *Dream Partner's Characteristics List.* This could be. However, unless you go ahead and make a decision on a partner, you will be doomed to a life of perpetual searching. If you keep waiting for the perfect person, then you will be waiting for a long, long time. Everyone has something about him or her that you are not going to like. It is up to you to decide whether or not you can live with those qualities that you don't appreciate. Give yourself a considerable amount of time to find a partner and then make a decision between your contenders. Just don't keep procrastinating about making the decision.

When it comes to things, such as intimacy, others have some emotional problems they need to face. Either they were children of divorce or they were very hurt, in the past, during another relationship. Many children of divorce report having a hard time with commitment because they have seen their family of origin break apart, which led them to conclude that there is no sense in making a commitment to something they believe will not last. Others hurt in past love relationships don't have the courage to make themselves vulnerable again. In both of these cases, the subjects have no real intention or strong desire for a committed love relationship. If they do find themselves in one, usually it will not be formalized into marriage because just the word "marriage" tends to make them break out with hives. They can live with partners, be committed to each other, remain sexually exclusive, and even raise children together. In essence, they can have a "marriage"; however, asking them to formalize it would send them into convulsions.

Some people have a higher tolerance for relationship ambiguity than others do. Are you one of those who have a high tolerance for a love relationship that is not a formal marriage? If you are in an arrangement that still provides you with all of your relationship needs, as well as commitment, then it's possible that you can be satisfied with a partner who has marital phobia. However, if you are like many others, in that you like to know where you stand in your relationships with others - especially your love partner - then you will probably be less tolerant of an undefined love relationship.

A formal marriage is not necessary to have a committed love relationship; however, it does have advantages. Marriage makes a statement to the rest of society that these two people are a union and that the rest of society is expected to respect this union. It makes a strong statement of commitment on the parts of both love partners. It is an official agreement between the love partners, one that says they are so committed to one another and their relationship that they are willing to make it legal and public.

This is why marriage commitments are stronger. They are public statements and legal agreements that say, "I intend to be with you and to provide for your needs until death do us part." When you marry someone, it provides him or her with a sense of security, a pledge that you can be trusted to be concerned with your partner's companionship needs. If you provide these needs without a formal marital commitment, then that's okay, but it does not provide the security that a public and legal statement does. Avoiding marriage gives love partners less reason to trust each other.

Think about it. In our society, all very important matters are handled with formal contracts. Houses, cars, major business transactions, and personal financial matters usually require formal agreements. None of these things is as important as your relationship with a love partner with whom you want to spend a major portion of your life. Think how you would feel if I entered into a business agreement with you, but when asked to sign a contract, I replied that I don't sign contracts. More than likely, you would start becoming suspicious of my trustworthiness and my intentions, concerning our relationship. The same is true with marriages. If you desire a formal marriage, but your potential partner is unwilling to do "the marriage thing," there is probably reason to question that potential partner's intent and trustworthiness. Contracts can and should be examined and negotiated for change. However, a person's complete avoidance of contracts really questions their commitment level.

There are other advantages to a legally binding marriage. In all relationships, there are rough times when a formal agreement and the hassles of voiding it give both partners time to cool off and think about whether the two of you really want to act on your impulses or work toward a solution. A second advantage is the extra measure of moral support a marriage receives from friends and family. No informal living arrangement ever receives quite the same measure of support and respect.

If you are ready for a serious, committed relationship and possibly even marriage, then you need to accept that desire and not settle for anything less. I have seen countless people wait years in a relationship with partners who had no intention or desire to rise to the level of commitment to a level that the other partner needed.

Naje, an attractive female in her mid-thirties, was very distraught. She had spent seven years with her boyfriend, Ricky, whom she loved very much. But he had procrastinated and continued putting off the formal commitment of marriage and starting a family. Naje was very upset because Ricky said he would be ready for marriage when he gets his promotion. When the promotion came, Ricky pushed the marriage date to some future date when he would become debt free. Once all bills were paid, the reason for postponement became his need to work through some emotional problems. From time to time, Ricky professed his readiness for marriage, but it was always at some future date, after he had successfully cleared another personal hurdle. This behavior drove Naje crazy with confusion. She loved Ricky and wanted to marry him. She believed he wanted to get married, too, but his actions told a different story. As I often share with my clients, one of the major truths I have learned is, when you notice someone's words and behavior contradicting each other, you should ignore what people say and pay attention to what they do. Actions, not only speak louder than words, they are also more honest.

After a while, Naje had had enough. She was ready to move on in her life, with or without Ricky. She wanted to have a husband and children, and she recognized that the longer she waited around for Ricky, her probability for having children decreased. I applauded her new resolution. Naje moved out of the apartment that she and Ricky shared and found her own place and told Ricky and his family that, unless he was ready to marry her, she was no longer going to be his girlfriend. Even though she missed Ricky, Naje began dating other people. She was being true to her self by not allowing Ricky to disrespect and use her anymore. Currently, Naje is in a new relationship that is progressing nicely.

When people get what they want from us but we do not get what we need in return, we are being disrespected. The old saying goes: "Why buy the cow if you can get the milk for free?" In other words, why should a person marry you if he or she is already getting everything he or she needs need from you? There is no motivation to marry you. Satisfied needs do not motivate. If you are in a relationship with someone who keeps putting off marriage and you know you are ready for this level of commitment, then you really need to consider leaving that person to fulfill your relationship needs. You will be glad you did, and whether that marriage-shy partner recognizes it or not, you are doing her or him a favor, as well. You will both be relieved from a relationship that is headed nowhere except towards more and more stress. Have the courage to change your course to *The Harmonious Way*. It can lead you to a partner who is mentally, physically, and spiritually in sync with you and your desires.

Money or Love

The legend of Midas, King of Phrygia, deals with the priority of money in our lives. As you may recall, one day King Midas was granted a single wish by the god called Bacchus. Midas was known for his strong desire for gold, and true to form, he wished that everything he touched would turn into gold. When Bacchus granted his wish, Midas was one happy king. As soon as he returned to his castle, he ordered his servants to prepare a celebration banquet. When he sat down to enjoy it, to his dismay, every morsel of food he touched turned to gold. He could neither eat nor drink anything set before him. When he went out into his garden to gather his thoughts, from her window his little daughter saw the king and rushed out to greet him. When Midas reached to give her a hug, the little princess turned into a statue of gold. No matter how hard he pleaded to Bacchus, the god would not reverse the "gift" Midas had been granted. Grief, starvation, and death awaited him in his golden world of glittering destruction.

Most young people today are concerned about their work careers, as they should be. But, career priority is often at the expense of establishing a primary love relationship. On their values list, career has a higher priority than finding a love partner. Sometimes people are lucky enough to find a compatible love partner, but if that person has a job that would take them away from their partner, too often the choice is to sacrifice the love relationship for the job. Such a sacrifice would be sad, but understandable, if it was made to follow a calling from God. However, unfortunately people often sacrifice love relationships for jobs that have nothing to do with their true passion or calling. They make the sacrifice strictly because the job offers more money. Talk about the cart before the horse!

Somewhere along the road of life's journey, we begin believing that money is more important than people. We forget that money is only a means, not an end. We forget that the money is to provide goods and services for our loved ones and ourselves. Money should be our servant and the servant of our loved ones, not our master. Money should not be the god of our lives to whom we sacrifice our love relationships on the altar of career. Even King Midas eventually recognized that the desire for gold is sometimes a curse that can prevent us from enjoying the simple pleasures of life and the love of a child or spouse.

Choosing the Right Contender

As you receive the information, you can fill out your *Potential Partner Chart*. As time goes by, you will accumulate more and more additional data and become increasingly able to tell if your initial assumptions are correct. The data will become more accurate as you get to know your potential partners. During the collection process, your data will enable you to zero in on one or two contenders. Contenders will help you narrow your focus and concentrate on your relationship with them.

Let's clearly define the word *contenders*. Contenders are the people on your list who (1) have more characteristics than others on your list, and (2) they are people you sense will be interested in a relationship with you. If a person has many characteristics on your list, but it is obvious that she or he is not interested in you, then you will be wasting your time trying to concentrate on growing that relationship. You want to concentrate on people you believe to be open to a relationship with you and have many of the characteristics that you are looking for in a partner.

I, again, remind you that you will, in all probability, never find someone who meets all of your characteristics, especially if you've taken this exercise seriously and have a substantial number of characteristics listed. The goal is to find someone with as many of your ideal characteristics as possible. All worthy contenders will not rack up a perfect score; so, I hope you can accept that fact and get on with the business at hand.

As mentioned in an earlier chapter, I used the processes of *The Harmonious Way* in my relationship shopping. True to form, I only dated women I considered physically attractive. But by the time I met Michelle, I had a characteristic list of 42 traits that I was looking for in a partner. Before every date I pulled out my list and read it. When I came home, I put in more work on my *Potential Partner Chart*.

I remember getting to the point where Michelle was the only one whom I classified as a contender. At the same time, I had also been seeing a woman we'll call Belinda. Belinda and I were attracted to each other immediately, and we had a lot of sexual chemistry. My relationship with Belinda was going much faster sexually than it was with Michelle. The only problem was Belinda did not score well on my *Potential Partner Chart* and stalled at a low number - even showing signs of sliding lower. On the other hand, Michelle's number of characteristics kept going higher.

Now the *old me* would have forgotten about Michelle and jumped into a relationship with Belinda. But the *new me* was tired of relationships not working out and accepted the fact that, if I wanted my life to change, then my decisions and behavior had to change. The *old me* would have been blinded by the sexual passion. The *new me* was wiser to the importance of compatibility in making a relationship work. The result: "bye-bye, Belinda... hello, Michelle." Looking back, I can see it was one of the best decisions I've ever made. I married Michelle, and we are enjoying our journey through life together as love partners, man and wife, and parents.

A friend asked us if I told Michelle about my analysis of her as a potential partner before we married, and we told him the answer was "yes." Then he asked Michelle what was her reaction when she learned about it? She said, "My reaction was basically the same as now. I thought it was a really good idea. In fact, in an unstructured way, I had been putting Aaron under the same microscope. I'll admit that some people might not like being looked upon in this way, the type person who expects their great love to come charging into their life on a white horse. I'd suspect that anyone who seriously took offense would be someone who had a low tolerance for reality and practicality."

Remember: You Are Choosing a Family, Too

When you marry someone you join with that person's family as well, especially if that potential partner is close to her or his family. So, when you are studying your potential partner, you should also be studying the family that comes in the deal and how your partner relates to each member. When you marry someone with children, you are taking on them as well. You are taking that potential partner's parents, siblings, and other relatives because they come as a package deal.

Mary and Donald both had children from previous marriages. When they married, she brought her daughter, Anna, to the blended household. Donald, who paid child support without complaint, did not have custody of his children; however, he looked forward to bringing them to his home on alternate weekends. But, there was one problem. Mary really didn't like this. Her ex-husband did not spend time with Anna nor did he pay child support; so, why should Donald? Mary just wanted it to be her daughter, her new husband, and no one else. Donald, on the other hand, treated Mary's daughter as if she was one of his own. However, when he brought his children over for the weekend, they were ignored and avoided by their new stepmother, and she complained if they spent more than the allotted time. Mary even started leaving with Anna to spend weekends with her mother, making Donald's children feeling slighted. Donald's anger grew week after week because he felt his children were being mistreated and that Mary was asking him to choose between her and his children.

Donald eventually chose. He now lives alone, except when his children come for the weekend. Often, he wonders why he can't seem to make his marriages work, gets depressed, and feels like a failure. Far from being a failure, I remind him that he is an inspiration. We talk about partner choices and marriage. I also applaud his dedication as a father. It is refreshing to see a responsible family man like Donald, even if that family is broken by divorce.

Don't make a potential partner choose between you and family. If her or his family is chosen, then you will miss out on having that person in your life. If you are chosen, then you may have won the battle, but lost the war. You'll have a partner, but the exclusion of our partner's family causes a subconscious rift that can manifest in your partner as depression, addiction, or resentment toward you.

A person's family is part of who she or he is. As you get to know a potential partner, observe and get to know the prospect's family as well. If you can't deal with your partner's family and friends, you might consider moving on to someone else.

Know Your Potential Partner's Bliss

I was amazed when Marsha, one of my clients, told me that her husband became very upset when she got into medical school. They attended college together and married shortly after graduation. Becoming a doctor had always been Marsha's dream, and even though she did not get immediately accepted into medical college, she had been persistent and eventually succeeded. When the letter of acceptance arrived, her husband did not share her excitement and joy. Eventually he admitted that, even though she had always talked about becoming a doctor, he never really thought she would actually get accepted for med. school. Now that she had, he did not want to be with her anymore.

You must allow your partner to pursue his or her bliss, the thing in life that gives your partner a sense of joy or purpose. Just as you are choosing a family, in addition to your partner, you are also choosing the pursuit of the partner's bliss. Do not get in the way because, if you do, you may be getting in the way of that person's calling. Rather than getting in the way or suggesting they give up their bliss because it is inconvenient for you or would allow them to make more money, try to encourage your partner by being supportive. If you don't, how can you expect your partner to be respectful and supportive of the pursuits that mean so much to you?

Yes, money is necessary, and both parties in a relationship are often responsible for bringing in the income needed to assure a family's survival. It is up to each partner to be understanding and supportive enough to carry an unequal portion. Sometimes one may carry all of the financial income load, while the other partner goes to school, has a baby, writes a book, raises the kids, starts a business, pursues a goal, or enjoys a hobby. This type of support is one of the greatest advantages of having a love partner. The main thing is to be fair in this support. Both partners should be encouraged to follow their bliss. And, the couple should work together to realize these dreams, while bringing in money and running a household at the same time. Each partner has the right to pursue his or her dream, but each partner also has the responsibility to do the unwelcome, yet necessary, tasks survival requires.

I hope you will talk a great deal with your potential partner about your bliss, dreams, and things you enjoy before committing to a lifetime together. You must be honest enough with yourself and ask whether or not you will be able to coexist with this person's movement toward personal goals that may not be yours?

Even though I did not become a pastor, at one time in my life I was very serious about doing so. Several of the women I dated liked me, but they really could not see themselves as a pastor's wife; so, they really saw no future in our relationship and would not allow a relationship to grow. Though this was frustrating for me as a young man, I now appreciate the women who were honest enough not to play games and aborted our relationship before it could become too serious.

Beware of Long Distance Romances

You can try having a long distance relationship if you wish. But, if you are looking for a committed, long-term relationship, I advise against adding the complication of long distance to the relationship equation. I have seen many cases where this type of scenario did not work out, including my own. Before my first marriage, my future wife and I had a long distance relationship. I was in California; she was in Georgia. We wrote each other, called each other, and visited each other as much as possible. But nothing beats spending time together and on a regular basis. Short romantic interludes are not an adequate substitute. They may be fun because the partners are totally focused on each other and are in the middle of the emotional drama of frequently having to say good-bye and missing each other greatly. The relationship vacillates from periods of yearning and separation to a lot of fun, sex, and good times crammed into brief times together. It isn't that difficult to put your best foot forward during these limited times together. However, when you finally end up living with each other every day, the glamour tends to fade. It's hard to play the part of the "ideal partner" round the clock, rather than be your real self.

But don't just take my word for it; there are some other cases to consider: Gary and Nora, for example. They began their marriage with a beautiful wedding. Gary was a physician in Atlanta; Nora was an attorney in Seattle. Their living conditions remained the same even after the marriage. Another example: Erica was a graduate student in the U.S., and her husband was in the military overseas. Neither couple's marriage lasted over two years. The last I heard, Erica is the only one who has remarried. These are just two of many more cases that I could cite, and you probably know of a number of similar failed arrangements. On the other hand, you may prove to be the rare exception and able to make a long distance relationship work. But why put yourself through the logistical hassle? If you are looking for full-time love, then don't waste your time with part-time partners.

Take Control of Your Love Life

The Harmonious Way's method of mate selection may seem somewhat cold and calculated to many of you who read this. I can hear you saying, Where is the "falling in love and romance?" I submit to you that the reason this method works is because it is more calculated than dependence on emotional whims and infatuation.

Rather than promoting "falling" in love, *The Harmonious Way* recommends "walking" into love. When you fall, you are usually out of control and usually end up getting hurt. Our culture tends to romanticize falling in love as an ideal, and our divorce rates prove it to be a gamble with poor odds. Falling in love entails making important life-changing decisions based on drama, emotion, infatuation, and other unconscious mechanisms that we do not control. We usually spend more conscious effort deciding where we will go on vacation or what car we will buy than we do on love partner selection. Among buying a car, going on vacation, and choosing a love partner, I think it is safe to say that choosing a love partner has more influence on our lives than the rest of the list.

Walking into love is a more sober approach to choosing a love partner. Walking into love is more rational and more conscious. It recognizes that true love is something that slowly grows, rather than a haphazard random piercing of our heart by fictitious Cupid's arrow. It also recognizes that your choice of a love partner is too important to leave it up to the weak decision-making processes we find in falling in love." You have the power to create your world. You have the power to create your love life and make it a rich, beautiful, and fulfilling experience while you are here on earth. Don't forfeit this power in the name of romantic sentimentality. Embrace *The Harmonious Way* to finding a love partner and true love will embrace you in return.

Without trust, you are not able to give and receive the love that both of you have for each other.

Gary Zukav

Chapter 7

Love Maintenance

How to Love

There is a story of a man who had a dream. In his dream he went to Hell and everyone was sitting around a table that was filled with a feast for kings and queens. Each person had one hand tied behind his or her back and a giant awkward spoon hanging down in front. When each person tried to use the spoon to eat, it was too awkward and they were not able to get the food in their mouths. As soon as the spoon reached a person's mouth, the food would fall onto the floor. People began to moan and lament, and eventually they withered away. Then the man dreamed that he went to Heaven where, to his surprise, he found the same setting. People were gathered around a royal feast with one hand tied behind their backs and big awkward spoons hanging in front. However, the man noticed that the people in Heaven had smiles on their faces. He asked them why they were smiling? A woman at the table replied that they were all very full and content. The man could not resist asking how this could be when the eating arrangements seemed to be set up for failure? The woman explained that they were able to eat because they fed each other.

That's the nature of love. Ideally, love for another works for the welfare of that other person as if you were working for your own welfare. This is what Jesus meant when he instructed us to "Love thy neighbor as thyself." Love doesn't keep score of how many loving acts I've treated you with and how many loving acts you have treated me with. Love is attitudinal surrender to desiring wellness for those you claim to love.

My wife, Michelle, helped me to learn this lesson. Before she and I came together, I was at a point in my dating career where I was looking out for myself. Because of being taken advantage of in so many relationship situations, I decided to demand that my relationships be 50/50. This was fair and just, and it protected me from being taken advantage of, as I had been in the past. This score-keeping attitude became a nuisance in our relationship because, rather than abandoning myself to just loving my wife, I was keeping score and demanding that I be treated with what I needed from her. This often led to many arguments and statements such as, "Well, I did this for you, but you didn't do that for me." This type of arguing back and forth is not productive in building and maintaining a good love relationship. What is needed in situations, such as this, is a complete attitudinal shift.

Love requires that we focus on the needs of the other, rather than our own needs. When you do, the object of your affection feels loved, and you don't have resentment because you are not focusing on what needs of yours have not been met. Focusing on what we don't have inevitably leads to our feeling deprived and unhappy. Focusing on the needs of others is the way of love and creates a better world for us to live in.

Love your partner and let your partner love you. You should show your love by providing your partner's needs, but you should also allow your partner to love you and show that love through providing for your needs. Research has shown that people have positive feelings toward others as a result of doing favors for them. People have a need to love and be loved; it is who we are. If you or your partner deny the other, the two of you aren't going down the right road of relationship maintenance. Believe it or not, there are people who will do for others but will not allow people to do for them. These are love martyrs who do a good job loving but do a horrible job of allowing others to show their love for them. Love martyrs fail to recognize the need within the object of their affection. As a result, they choke their love relationships with one-way love.

When Sam came into my office for counseling, he was depressed because he had just broken up with his girlfriend Barbara. Sam and Barbara met at work and immediately felt a physical attraction toward each other. Their courtship was a thrill for both. Each was loving, and each made a conscious effort to do things for the other. When Sam did something special for Barbara, she was genuinely appreciative. However, when Barbara tried to treat Sam lovingly, he was appreciative but acted undeserving. She offered to treat him with gifts she knew he wanted and trips he longed to take, but he would refuse. As time went on, Sam was doing more for Barbara than Barbara was doing for Sam. He always called her and never really gave her a chance to call him first. Gradually Sam began to notice a change in Barbara. She seemed to be more withdrawn and to be taking Sam for granted. She became mean and short when talking with him, and as time progressed, Barbara eventually dumped him, leaving Sam devastated and bewildered. He thought that he had been the perfect boyfriend because he had shown his love for her the best he knew how.

Sam did love Barbara, but again we are shown that love is not enough. Sam loved Barbara but would not allow her to love him just as much. Our partner will not love us, if we behave as if we are unworthy of being loved. If you do not allow your partner to express love in return, your partner's respect for you will decrease. And why should you love someone you don't respect? An unbalanced love relationship will eventually turn the sweetest love partner into an aggressive monster, leaving the one who could not accept love telling everyone how unfair it was that his or her partner changed.

A happy, long lasting love relationship consists of mutual loving behavior. Mutual, because it must flow back and forth between the partners. Both must surrender themselves to an attitude of giving and receiving. I say loving behavior because the affective paradigm of love as a cozy, fond feeling about someone is too weak a foundation to build a relationship on. Under this affective paradigm, people allow themselves to behave as unlovingly toward partners as they please - yet still claim that they love their partners. Many of them truly value their partners; nonetheless, this type of lopsided love is not strong enough to sustain a lasting, healthy relationship.

To have a long lasting love relationship, love needs to have a behavioral paradigm rather than an affective paradigm. To put it another way, "Actions speak louder than words!" Our behavior needs to show that we value our partner. To love you, I need to communicate through my behavior that I value you.

We all have different values and things that we want and need from each other. Often when working with couples I have each partner list, say, five specific things that they want from their partner. If it were more than five it would be too overwhelming. The requests must also be specific. One woman said she wanted her husband to be more affectionate. This is a legitimate request, but it's too vague to expect results. If your partner doesn't know how to be more affectionate, he will probably give up trying and you will just get frustrated. A more specific version of this request would be something like, "Hug me three times a day," or "Say you love me at least once a day," or "Kiss me hello and good-bye."

I've also had a husband say that he wanted his wife to make more rational decisions about their finances. Too vague. A better version of this request would be something like, Include me on financial decisions that involve $200 or more."

This exercise has proven to be helpful for many, but it must be approached from a position of mutual respect for each other and the other's needs. It is not meant for you to argue about the needs of the other person. If a person has a certain request of you, it's not your place to judge their need as valid or invalid. If your partner's request doesn't harm anyone or cause any conflict with your moral convictions, then just shut up and give your partner what he or she wants. Love is giving people what they think they want and need - not what you think they really want or really need. If you remember this and use it as your guide in trying to behave lovingly with your partner, it will go a long way toward helping you have a happy relationship.

People can say that they love you until they are blue in the face, but unless the words are backed by actions, the words don't mean a thing. Make love a verb in your relationship and allow both of you to feel loved by the other. The following charts can help you in your attempts to love.

The Harmonious Way *LOVE NEEDS CHART*		
Name:	Needs from:	
1.		
2.		
3.		
4.		
5.		

The Harmonious Way *LOVE NEEDS CHART*		
Name:	Needs from:	
1.		
2.		
3.		
4.		
5.		

After you and your partner create your individual charts, swap them. Put the chart of your partner's needs somewhere you will automatically see it every day. This will serve as a constant reminder to demonstrate your love to your partner daily.

It is a good idea to repeat this exercise periodically because our wants and needs are always changing. My wife and I try to do this at least annually by incorporating each other's needs into our personal New Year's resolutions. If you do this, you may want to cut down your love needs to two or three so your partner can have room for his or her own personal goals for the year.

Equality

I cannot even begin to count the number of couples I have seen whose primary relationship disease was caused by an infection from a virus known as sexism. They are creeping and sometimes even going backwards from their desired destination of marital happiness. We are now in a new millennium, and there are men who still insist on doing things the old way. These men insist that the problem with marriages today is that men have lost control and are no longer the head of the household. The belief is that God ordained the male to rule over the female. As these husbands remain entrenched in their belief, citing Biblical authority, many of them cannot figure out why their wives are so unhappy.

Hellooo?! The wives are unhappy because they are being subjected to sexist treatment. In today's culture of dual career families in which both the wives and the husbands go out and make money, the women are still expected to do most of the housework, cook, and submit to their husband's authority. Even if the wives do not have a career outside the home, they usually still take care of the household. This is a full time job in itself, and it is usually minimized and receives no gratitude or fanfare. So, the females usually not only carry more than their share of the weight of responsibility; they also are expected to let the man have the final authoritative word on family behavior.

This type of relationship is not a partnership. It is a dictatorship that dominates females and steals their joy of living. Some men may claim that this type of paternalistic love is benevolent; however, the behavior it produces is becoming less and less palatable for the women of today. This is why many females claim to be happier when they are not in a relationship. Household chores are an area of concern in many homes, a hot topic that leads to frequent arguments. When our roles were defined along gender lines, this was not so much an issue for debate. The male went out and earned money; the female stayed home and ran the household. There is nothing inherently wrong or right about such an arrangement. If it still works for your relationship, then you have no need to change. However, many households today are dual career families. This means that the male and the female both go out and earn money. The problem that often arises is the female shares the traditionally male responsibility of breadwinner, but the male doesn't share the traditionally female responsibility of household chores. This puts an enormous burden on the female. In fairness, let me add that, today, I am seeing an increase in the dual career families where the man is the one taking on most of the household chores.

Another very different dynamic is one in which one partner works, while the other partner lounges during the day, spending time shopping, watching soap operas and talk shows, or playing video games. In some cases the lounger is female, in others it's the male. In either case, inequality in a relationship builds resentment.

My wife and I have had our share of arguments over the years, concerning household chores. We are a dual career family, and each of us was perceiving that the other was not pulling his/her share of the load. After many years of arguing and bickering about this subject, it finally occurred to us to write down all of the household chores and to come to an agreement, concerning who would be responsible for what, and when, then put the responsibility list on our refrigerator. We've found the responsibility list or what I call here *The Harmonious Way* Chore Chart to be quite helpful. I'm certain you'll find it to be a great peacemaker.

The Harmonious Way *CHORE CHART*

Place your or your partner's name in the space for a particular chore on a particular day.
Warning! You and your partner must complete this chart together.

Chore	Mon.	Tues.	Wed.	Thurs.	Fri.	Sat.	Sun.
Kitchen							
Bathrooms							
Vacuum							
Garbage							

As long as we hold onto sex role stereotypes and refuse to treat each person as an individual with different strengths and needs, we will continue being plagued by sexism in marriage. There is an interstate road that will get you to your destination of marital happiness very quickly; it's called equality. Holding on to sexist beliefs will only leave you frustrated and far away from your goal of a happy relationship.

Communication

Here it is. I know you were waiting for this section. It is an unwritten rule that all relationship books are required to at least mention the importance of communication. Yes, communication is very important. The benefit of a love relationship is intimacy. Intimacy is difficult to have without good communication. You can live with someone in a small, one-room apartment, but if you don't communicate with each other, you can still be very lonely.

Communication allows us to express ourselves to another soul. If we are not criticized or judged when we expose ourselves, then the communication becomes an affirming experience. But, just talking to someone is not enough. The listener has to provide evidence that he or she understands what we are talking about. This is why it's a good idea for you and your partner to speak the same language. Even if you do speak the same language, you need to have enough in common so that your partner can fully participate in conversing with you on certain topics. However, you do not have to talk with your partner about all topics. If the two of you communicate well, concerning topics such as your children, your jobs, and your relationship with friends, then don't get all bent out of shape if your partner is not interested in talking about sports or fashion or whatever your favorite pastime may be. If you have good communication about world events and real estate investing, then don't go nuts if your partner is not interested in spiritual topics or modern art. These topics can be explored with others. There is nothing wrong with communicating with other people in your life about topics in which you and your partner don't share interest. You can have this type of psychological intimacy with others without overloading your partner by expecting her or him to be everything to you and to fulfill your every need. That's far too much of a burden to place on one person. So communicate with your partner on topics of mutual interest, and find other friends who enjoy talking about the things that your partner has no interest in. Your partner may pretend that he or she is interested in some topics when that is not really the case. One way to tell is to observe her or him while you talk. If your partner lapses into the blank stare of a zombie, it's time to find someone else for the topic of conversation you are pursuing.

Communication is a good thing, and the more you share with your partner about what is going on inside you, the closer your relationship will be. However, contrary to what many will advise, I do suggest a limit to your communication with your partner. There are certain things that are best kept to yourself. There is such a thing as too much information. If you sometimes fantasize about others when you are making love to your partner, it is probably not a good idea to mention it. If there is a friend, co-worker, or someone in your partner's family who sexually attracts you, sharing that is not advised. It is also not a good idea to talk about your past sexual experiences with other partners beyond the fact that you had them. Any more detail can prove to be too much information.

This is not a hard and fast rule, but you do want to be careful. Even though your partner may invite you to share such thoughts, human egos have a hard time dealing with even fantasy competition, and your partner may become more insecure, causing your relationship to become unnecessarily stressed. Different couples have different tolerance levels for this type of communication. Some people get very upset if they even see their partner so much as noticing someone else. My wife and I have a little more tolerance. We are able to point out strangers whom we find sexually attractive, and we are comfortable sharing this with each other. However, we tend not to express how we feel about people we know because that could feel threatening. Nothing is going to happen between you and a total stranger seen walking down the street, but a close acquaintance or co-worker with whom you frequently come in contact, well, that could be another matter. Other couples may even have abundant tolerance and not be bothered by the sexual thoughts and feelings their partners have toward others. Still, the safest bet is not to push your luck. And, of course, just because you feel sexual attraction toward someone other than your partner, it does not mean you should act on it.

On most subjects, we definitely should communicate. Clear communication is the lifeblood of every relationship. Your partner needs to hear how much you love and value her or him. And even though it may not be comfortable for either of you to state your anger, hurts, and fears, they should be expressed, too, so that they won't grow to unmanageable proportions.

Risk Arguing

Arguing is a form of communication that isn't always a bad thing. And, expressing your thoughts and feelings may trigger an argument. The more compatible you and your partner are, the more harmonious your relationship will be. The more harmonious your relationship, the less tension you will experience. The less tension in your relationship, the less cause for arguing. The more incompatible you are the more tension and arguments you and your partner will have. Obviously, having a partner with whom you are never inclined to argue seems ideal; but is that really the case?

Let's say tension builds up over some issue. The question is what do you do with that tension? It has been my experience with couples that it is best to express tensions. Doing so will often lead to bickering and arguing. This is why many people prefer not to express their tension because they have a low tolerance for arguing and disagreements. Arguments and disagreements are not a sign that your relationship or marriage is over. It is just a sign of existing tension. This tension is not the problem. Problems can result, however, when the tension is not handled appropriately. If you choose to express your tension, there is hope, because it shows that you are willing to move toward bridging the chasm created by your differences. If you choose to withdraw and not express your feelings, then your relationship is probably headed for trouble.

I remember visiting some friends of the family and spending the night at their house. I had known this couple for years, and they had been married for over fifty years. That visit was an eye opener because, by spending the night with them, I got to see the amount of arguing and bickering they did. I had never seen it before. The interesting thing about it was they had been happily married for over fifty years, were very close to one another, and loved each other dearly. Many couples from the outside looking in would probably say, Why don't they just get a divorce?" On the contrary, this couple knew how to relate. The couples that don't argue are the ones that are scary because they are not relating. They have chosen withdrawal instead. They have chosen to be housemates and nothing more.

In counseling, I meet many newly married couples who genuinely care for each other; however, they can not accept the reality of arguing. They expect things to be calm and serene "round the clock. First of all, if you are choosing *The Harmonious Way* to find a love partner, there will be less tension. However, arguing is inevitable, unless you have found your exact clone as a potential partner. Arguing is simply inevitable because no two people are the same. When you marry you become a union, a union with two different brains. And, where you have two different brains there will be two different mindsets.

Arguing is not necessarily a bad thing. Arguing is a sign that you are really getting out some things that need to be said; some true feelings and frustrations are being expressed. If you don't argue, it means one of two things: (1) you and your partner are exactly alike, or (2) the two of you don't communicate very much.

In my first marriage, we hardly ever argued, but as peaceful as the apartment was, the relationship was in ruins. Today, with a weird sort of pride, I can say that my wife and I do our fair share of arguing. And I might add, usually before the night is over we have made up, and things are back to normal. If you don't argue and let hurts and frustrations steep in your mind, you are putting your relationship in danger because the unexpressed emotions are the dangerous ones. You'll end up saying, But, we never argued; how could our relationship go wrong?"

One reason many are afraid to argue is because they know that arguing can take a turn for the worst. This is possible: so, you want to make sure you have a third eye watching and monitoring your behavior, as you engage in bickering. There are two major things to look and listen for. If you or your partner begin to engage in personal insults, rather than arguing about the issues, then you are crossing the line into unhealthy arguing. If this happens, I suggest you come to some type of agreement not to "go there" when you are in disagreement with each other. If it continues to occur, I suggest that you get some couples counseling.

Another sign of unhealthy arguing is physical violence. If you or your partner intentionally harm each other physically, then your relationship is in big trouble. It may still be salvageable after only one or two occurrences, but this type of behavior is unacceptable, and even one or two occurrences needs to be seriously discussed and considered grounds for entering into a counseling relationship with a professional. Never let your relationship become abusive. Better to withdraw from each other and not communicate than to allow violence. Frequent occurrences of verbal and especially of physical abuse serve as a sign that the relationship needs to come to an end, at least temporarily if not permanently. When loving *The Harmonious Way*, relationships are supportive and creative, not dysfunctional and destructive.

Again, arguing can be a good thing, if it leads to clearer communication and solutions that are acceptable to both parties. Periodic arguing can build mutual trust in the strength of your union, if you both listen and both work towards a positive resolution - even if that resolution is to agree to disagree on a particular issue. Arguing that is not abusive is certainly not as harmful as the silent alternative.

Trust

This is a big one. When you commit to your partner, you are making a statement that you are trustworthy and that your partner can depend on you for honesty and support. The importance of trust can be depicted most strongly in the requirement of sexual exclusivity that exist in most committed relationships and marriages and in the consequences of having this trust broken.

Sexual Trust

We may relate to others and spend time and money on others, but, if we have sexual intercourse with someone other than our partner, we tread on dangerous territory. Even if you and your partner haven't said it to one another in so many words, you are rare, indeed, if you do not expect sexual exclusivity from each other. Sexual exclusivity is the normal expectation in our society. When one or both parties moves outside of a monogamous relationship, a strong sense of betrayal arises and adds much complexity.

During the late 1960's and early 1970's, a concept and practice became popular known as "open marriages." This basically allowed for secondary sexual relationships outside of the primary marital relationship. The alleged virtue of open marriages was that it was based on an agreement between the two partners. Even today there are couples married and unmarried who participate in "swinging". Swingers have sex separately or together with other couples. Again, the professed virtue in this practice is that it is "above board" and is not an exercise in deception or a betrayal of trust.

Despite the utopian appeal of this liberal sexual lifestyle, there are many risks involved that make it too dangerous for most. An unwanted pregnancy could result. Contracting sexually transmitted diseases becomes more probable. The love relationship becomes more complex and more vulnerable to attacks from each partner's insecurity and jealousy. All risk levels accelerate. Many couples who experiment with liberal sexual lifestyles discover they are not fulfilling for them. As one friend told me, "When my marriage 'opened up,' it also fell apart."

The first question you should ask yourself is not whether this practice is either right or wrong; here's the big question: is it right for my relationship with this particular partner? After you've answered the big question, you can decide what your answer is to the other.

Of those people who hanker for sex outside of their primary relationship, most do not practice these sexually open lifestyles. Instead, they either keep their partner's trust by remaining sexually monogamous, or they betray their partner's trust and have secret affairs. When the non-cheating partner discovers the betrayal, a great amount of trust is lost. The relationship may or may not continue because one of the partners betrayed the trust, and the other will find that difficult to forget.

Staying Sexually Loyal: Flee Temptation

And it came about after these events that his master's wife looked with desire at Joseph, and she said, "Lie with me.' But he refused. And it came about as she spoke to Joseph day after day, that he did not listen to her to lie beside her, or be with her. Now it happened one day that he went into the house to do his work, and none of the men of the household was there inside. And she caught him by his garment saying, "Lie with me!' And he left his garment in her hand and fled, and went out-

Genesis 39: 7-12 NAS

Why did Joseph flee? There are many people who sincerely love their spouses and children. But they strongly desire to have sexual relationships with others. This is why I believe it is false for my fellow psychologist to label partners who sexually stray as mentally ill. There are many happy marriages and families that are unaware of the outside sexual relationships of their partners. However, keeping such a secret is extremely stressful for the individual that is "creeping." If the creeping spouse goes beyond having superficial sexual affairs and forms a love relationship with another, then the primary marriage becomes a certain target for problems. It has to compete with an outside force that requires time, energy, and money from the creeper. This means there will be less of these resources for the cheater's family.

The best way to keep your marriage free from too much jealousy and stress is to remain sexually loyal. Monogamy is simply less complex. And, unless you and your spouse have agreed on a sexually open marriage, when you have sex with others, you will constantly have to live with the knowledge that you are lying to and deceiving the ones you love.

There are not many of us who can honestly say they have not been attracted to people other than their spouse. Most of us, at different times during our marital life, have experienced temptation. And, if we sense the other party is also having feelings similar to ours, the attraction can become very powerful. Therefore, a *defining moment* is created. A defining moment is one in which you are forced to choose one value over another.

There are many situations in life where we can avoid choosing one value over another. If we are creative enough, we can usually find some way to have our cake and eat it, too. But in defining moments, no amount of finessing can make the two values peacefully coexist. Pertaining to the topic at hand, Either I sleep with this person, or I remain sexually loyal to my partner." The obvious logical choice for us to make is to remain sexually loyal because to choose otherwise can greatly complicate our lives. Notice I said *logically*. The obstacle for making such a logical choice is the presence of sexual lust. Lust is very intoxicating.

Let's say that even though you have a strong sweet tooth, you've just sworn off sweets and are committed to a new, healthy diet. The very next day you are invited by a friend to go to an all-you-can-eat party at a dessert bar. What we have here is a defining moment. Which value is a higher priority: the benefits of your diet or the temporary pleasure of consuming the desserts? Logically you would choose the benefits of your diet. You convince yourself that you can go to the bar just to hang with friends. But, when you get there, the sights and smells of the pastries, doughnuts, ice cream, cakes, pies, and cookies start getting to you. You will more than likely start to become intoxicated by a lust for these things. You do pretty well for a little while. Then, you decide that it couldn't hurt to just taste that chocolate cake your friend is raving about. So, you taste a piece and remark how good it is. You're okay. There is no guilt because one little taste is no big deal. But, the stimulation becomes too much, and you become drunk with desire. Logic flies out the window, and you find yourself saying, "To hell with it, I'll get back on my diet tomorrow!" Once you finished bingeing on the sweet lover's feast, the two-headed monster of guilt and low self-esteem enters, and you ask yourself, *"Why did I do it?"* The answer: *lust intoxication.*

The dessert party story is not a "devil made me do it" explanation - much less justification - for continued sexual infidelity. However, it is an illustration of a decision-making process that can cause us to make choices that are not congruent with our priorities and, therefore, not in our best interest. While lust intoxication over sweets could be hazardous to our physical health, sexual lust can be hazardous to our social relationships.

One secret to succeeding in a battle against lust is early intervention. The sooner you evacuate the temptation zone, the easier it is for you to resist. The longer you allow your intoxication level to rise, the harder it is to emerge victorious. That's why it's best not to allow yourself to get into certain situations. In other words, if you are on a diet, don't go to a dessert bar. If you find yourself sexually attracted to a person besides your spouse, you may want to keep your interactions with that person on a lighthearted, superficial level. If you feel yourself strongly attracted, consider actually avoiding that person, especially if you sense the attraction is mutual. The earlier you recognize temptation and the earlier you remove yourself from it the better. Even if you have to literally run away from it. That is why Joseph fled.

Don't Get Horny

One other secret that will help you stay sexually loyal is not allowing yourself to get horny. If you allow yourself to get horny, you will be more sensitive to sexual temptation. How does one keep from getting horny? The best way is to have sex frequently with your partner. There is no magic number of times per week or month. Don't let anybody try to convince you that there is. Just keep in mind to fulfill your sexual needs regularly with each other. If you start feeling horny, then that is a good clue that maybe you are overdue for some sexual recreation with your partner. Not only will this help you stay loyal, but also it does wonders in building your feelings of closeness and intimacy with one another.

Some complain that sex gets boring after having it frequently with the same person. If you and/or your partner are among the complainers, do some things to spice up your sex life. Go to an adult novelty store together and shop for clothes, toys, and media that might peak your interest. Try different positions, rooms, or locations. Buy mirrors. People who have partners who take care of themselves by staying physically fit tend to be happier with their sex lives. So, do yourself and your partner a favor by getting and staying in shape. You are only limited by your own imagination. As long as you and your partner are in agreement and no one gets hurt, then there is no limit to the sexual adventures that you and your partner can experience together.

Sing and dance together and be joyous, but let each one of you be alone, Even as the strings of a lute are alone though they quiver with the same music.

- Kahlil Gibran

Chapter 8

Becoming A Harmonious Chord

True intimacy is sharing your soul with your partner. It's allowing the God in you to commune with the God in your partner. It's a blissful feeling of oneness in the midst of your individuality. The following pages explore how to have intimacy in your relationship.

It's important that you spend quantity and quality time together with your partner. One without the other just won't do. Sitting down watching television together without uttering a word to each other the whole evening is quantity time. However, it lacks quality. Going on vacation together for one week a year might be quality. But you need more to keep a relationship going the rest of the year. The more time you spend together, the more you become a harmonious chord. You need to be involved together. Your partner deserves priority over your other relationships.

During your time together, give each other mental and physical intimacy. Intimate moments can go a long way in building a relationship. Intimate moments are times when you and your partner are concentrating your attention and energy on each other. We have so much to compete with today. Television, reading material, music, the Internet, outside organizations, family, and friends are all pulling on us for our attention. After a long day at work, you may just want to plop down in front of the television and veg" out. The partner, whom you say you love and care about, ends up with a tired version of you, while the rested, fresh you is given to the job.

Do your best to schedule some time with family. I try to devote Sundays to mine. You may prefer to more evenly distribute your family time throughout the week. The main point is not to leave your spouse or children off your calendar. Still, make sure that the kids go to bed on schedule so that you and your partner have time to focus on each other and share how the day went. Who knows, you may have some time for some sexual intimacy, as well?

The more quality time you spend with each other, the more you should be able to notice your mutual love growing and changing. Your love will start to look more like a strong friendship and less like a romantic love story.

Being in a love relationship is sacramental. Experiencing God goes beyond rituals and spiritual exercises. We experience Him in our everyday lives, even if we don't always recognize it as such. Feeling loved and affirmed is knowing God's grace and presence. The counseling relationship, a friendship, or a love relationship can all be sacramental to the point that they allow us to receive God's kindness. Even walking down the street and having a stranger smile and say "hello" is a brief sacramental moment. We are all expressions of God and have the ability to deliver God's grace to each other. The next time you gaze into your partner's eyes, remember that you are seeing a person possessed by God. Recognizing this also helps us treat each other more lovingly.

A love relationship can be a particularly strong sacrament. It is probably why most of us want to experience having one. A love relationship is so strong because it is a relationship in which two vessels of God come together and commune on a very intimate level. The more intimate in body and soul, the more powerful the sacramental experience. The act of physical touch can be very affirming. The most powerful version of this type of physical affirmation is sexual intercourse. The act of sexual intercourse is so powerful that this communal event of bringing two expressions of God together is a vehicle in which God can create a human being. Our souls can experience the grace of God through honest communication and having shared lives with one another. There is something very secure in being able to depend on another individual to be there for you in your time of need.

The symphony of Love has many notes. You are called to play yours, and I am called to play mine. We are different notes; however, as we spend our lives together intimately, we gradually become one harmonious chord. This allows us to play beautiful music together, while staying true to our own note.

The feeling of oneness is sacred because it brings us closer to the reality of the oneness of all creation. We are not required to have a love partner to experience the oneness of God, but it's a precious gift from Him that allows us a glimpse of God's nature.

......As I put the finishing touches on this section, my wife is pregnant with twins and still asleep upstairs. I am in my office, being interrupted by my five-year old daughter trying to talk to me. It is quite frustrating, but as I look into her eyes, I can't get angry. I couldn't possibly because, in her eyes, I recognize the answer to a prayer prayed by a young man from a bathroom floor in California one November night, years ago.

No one can serve two masters; for either he will hate the one and love the other, or he will hold to one and despise the other. You cannot serve God and mammon... But seek first His Kingdom and His righteousness; and all these things shall be added to you.

-- Matthew 6:24, 33. NAS

Chapter 9

Extending
The Harmonious Way™
into Friendships, Family, and Career

he Harmonious Way applies to virtually every aspect of your life. It's the process of defining and accepting your personal identity, identifying your ideal, systematically identifying an excellent match, and working towards a goal of on-going harmony. It works because it's based on the creation of harmony for both you and for others. I am assuming that you have read the first portion of this book and that you are well aware that a brief description of a step is like describing the entrance to a gold mine. The deeper you go, the greater the riches to be found. With that said, let's begin applying *The Harmonious Way* to aspects of your life, other than love partnership.

Friends and Family

If you want to have harmonious relationships with others, then set yourself up for success. Relate to people with whom you have the most in common. Forced relationships can be a strain and are often unnecessary. Once you have spent the time necessary to figure out who you are, then you are able to determine which people you should relate to on a regular basis.

I know someone who says we only need seven close friends. I'm not certain how he came up with this number. The maximum who can sit around a dinner table and share the same conversation with you? The comfortable number to fit in two cars for a trip somewhere? No matter how he goes about doing his math, he has a point; we don't require scores of close relationships to be happy. In fact, none of us has the time required to develop dozens and dozens of close relationships.

My parents live on a small private lake. When some of my friends discovered this, they asked me if I enjoy fishing? I like fishing well enough, but it's not something I live to do; so, and I told them that fishing was okay - but not something I did very often.

I've learned to be clearer in my replies because, until I did, friends would quickly ask to be invited to go fishing at the lake. That meant I had to set aside time I would have preferred spending on other activities for a day swatting mosquitoes and baiting hooks. Part of me enjoyed the time with friends, but a larger part of me became annoyed at spending my valuable gift of life doing something that I do not want to do. There was work piling up on my desk - not to mention activities I would have enjoyed taking a break to share with friends. However, there was no longer time to do the things I would have preferred, thanks to the fishing trips.

It's not really recreation unless you are having a good time. But if you are going to do something, why not do something you enjoy? Then the cost of putting off things you need or want to do is not as expensive. This certainly applies to friendships. If your friends want to go fishing this week while you do something else, there's nothing wrong with that. Tell them you hope they catch the limit. You can get together with them the following week for something all of you like to do.

When I take time out to spend with family and friends at a party or over dinner, I welcome these interruptions in my schedule. Where would be the joy in life if we do not take time to spend with the ones we love? Isn't this the reason we spend so many hours making money in the first place? Most of us work to be able to afford the things that bring us pleasure. Spending time with a friend, doing things that you both enjoy is the ideal. Doing something that only one of you enjoys can become a burden and bring a negative association into the friendship.

We cannot choose our family, and we cannot always choose our acquaintances, the people with whom we spend time at work or associate with in civic or religious organizations. But, to the extent that you can, I highly recommend that you choose to relate to others with whom you have many things in common. This enriches your life and makes it more fulfilling. Furthermore, it does the same for theirs.

I'm in no way saying that people should do away with their present friendships or dissolve family relations. If you have people in your life that you love and care about, even though you do not have much in common with them, give some thought to the matter. Find something you do have in common with these people and relate to each other in that arena - not the arena of dissimilarities.

I'll call them "the Joneses." They are a couple my wife and I like very much, and all of us have a great deal in common. We share a love of the same sports, enjoy many of the same types of books and movies, and have children of similar ages and in the same school. However, our mutual commonality stops short when it comes to the matter of religious beliefs. During the early part of our relationship with the Joneses, they frequently invited us to worship services and other activities at their congregation. We enjoyed fellowship with our friends but were not comfortable in their religious environment, which is a big part of their lives. The same is true for my wife and me; so, we were not willing to pretend that we were comfortable in their house of worship. To pretend otherwise was living a lie. Eventually, I worked up enough courage to express my religious beliefs to the husband. Fortunately, he and his wife were diversity mature enough to accept this difference; consequently, the four of us maintain a close friendship outside of the religious arena.

Speaking of friendships between couples, sometimes there may be a situation where your spouse or partner has a friend whom you do not particularly care for or you do not enjoy being around the friend's partner. Rather than force your relationship with these people, I suggest that you encourage your love partner to have some free time away from you to spend with these people. You should not be forced into disharmony, and your partner should not give up harmonizing with others just because your note doesn't fit in a particular chord. The solution? It's a simple one.

Don't gripe when your spouse or partner wants to spend time with his/her friends. As long as you are priority number one in your love relationship and your intimacy needs are being met by the one you love, then let your partner interact with others without having to drag you along all the time - especially when it's not your type of crowd. If you force it and try to fit into what are inharmonious environments for you, your discomfort will show. Not only will you have a miserable time; you may turn what could be an enjoyment for the rest into a disappointment for everyone involved.

This dynamic can happen in families, as well. If you think for a moment, I doubt that it will take you long to think of a family member who is not on your list of favorite folks. However, because you are related, the two of you are forced to interact at family gatherings. These situations can be a strain and take more work. Don't ignore these relatives. Instead, interact with them only within areas of non-contention. Everyone deserves respect and civility. Let's say the two of you hold strong, opposing political views. Well, it's a free country; each of you has a right to believe what you wish. However, a family reunion is not the best place to butt heads over matters of politics. If you care enough about the family member, you can try to develop the relationship by searching for a commonality or shared point of view. Maybe you are both fans of the same sports team or like discovering new Mexican restaurants or are into family genealogy or a dozen other subjects. No matter how short the list, it should give you enough conversational fodder to get you through your occasional times together comfortably, harmoniously.

You can even discuss areas of contention, if you are brave enough to risk arguing. Sometimes such discussions can lead to a closer relationship. Of course, they can also underscore your incompatibility with each other. If relationship-building efforts continue to fail, you do not have to avoid family gatherings. Just continue to maintain your respect and civility toward the troublesome family member, but do not feel obligated to take up the cross of forced family harmony. True harmony is not forced. Everyone does not have to be best of friends, even in families. Play your note and let each family member play hers or his. If you are not in harmony with someone, more than likely noise will be produced instead of music. A certain amount of noise can be tolerated; however, if it is too noisy, feel free to retreat for a while to another auditorium. You will be doing everyone a favor.

Career

If you are unhappy at work, you are not alone. Many people find their careers great disappointments and feel they are stuck, from 9:00 to 5:00 in jobs that don't allow them to be who they really are.

Why do we do it to ourselves? Most of us say, I have no choice," or This is the only thing I know." Some of us chose our occupations with only one thought in mind: the choice seemed to be a good, prudent economic decision, one that could provide a comfortable livelihood. But, is that reason enough for you to dedicate your life to a particular career path?

I have personally struggled with this issue. When I was a youngster and an adult would ask me, What do you want to be when you grow up, Aaron?", my usual reply was, I'm going to be a "medical doctor."
Was this a well thought out career decision? No. It was a decision made by my parents, a decision I adopted to please them. And, to be brutally honest, when I responded so confidently with such a respected occupation, adults were quite impressed.

Eventually, during my teens, the idea of being in school all those years really turned me off, and I came to the realization that I did not want to be a physician. Worse still, I didn't know what I wanted to be. This created a problem because I could no longer answer with the confidence I once did, and adults were not at all impressed by my ambiguity.

There was another tug on me. The high school I attended was very intent on channeling its best students toward engineering; so, I went with the flow. Engineering then became "my" career choice. Once again, I was free of pressure because the adults had returned to being pleased and impressed with my response to the "when you grow up" question.

Then came college. I entered an engineering program, and while the grades I earned were okay, in my heart and mind, I wasn't. I was miserable. I had no interest whatsoever in the hard sciences, and it was killing me on the inside. For a couple of years, I had been traveling fast on my own spiritual journey, and by my freshman year in college, I knew that I felt called to be a minister. I clearly remember the night I phoned my parents to tell them of my change in plans. To my amazement, they were not surprised by my decision and said they knew deep down that I was on a spiritual track. Nonetheless, my mom and dad, the sponsors of my education, were intent on providing me a financial safety net. So, we struck a bargain. We agreed that, if I majored in business, it would give me enough extra hours to take the religion courses I was eager to take. I reluctantly chose business as a compromise, tolerated the business courses, and paid my dues. But, when it came to my religious classes, I devoured them with a voracious appetite, seldom making less than an A on any assignment or exam.

Eventually I was able to follow my bliss. I went to seminary, then proceeded to graduate school, where I studied counseling. During my time as a student, studying counseling, I became a father. That's when a major sense of responsibility overcame me. I began worrying that I would not be able to provide an adequate living for my family. Gradually, my major career question became *How can I make money?* - instead of *What is my calling?* That's when I began considering career paths based on monetary gain rather than who I was.

Fortunately for me, I got back on track. Through my career counseling courses, my teaching experience, counseling, and being supervised, I began to recognize the value of staying true to myself in my work life. I now try to stay focused on my purpose in life and my particular mission while I am here. I try to keep in touch with who I am and where I can comfortably express myself in the world of work.

I've counseled countless students who have been coerced into their career paths. Either their parents pressured them into making an unwelcome choice, or they coerced themselves with worries about their financial future. Many of these students were distressed; some were so distressed that they even contemplated suicide. Frequently by the time they come to counseling, most were too close to graduating to change their majors. Such situations usually result in resignation to careers that prove unfulfilling. It seems that the lack of faith in God or the Universe to provide for us leads us to sell out. We sell our souls and potential fulfillment for money or security. So, on we go, living our lives, not truly being who we are created to be, pretending to like our jobs, wearing masks, and hiding our true natures. Again, the culprit is fear. This time it is the fear of poverty or fear of losing the respect of others. Do you have a close relationship with this type of fear?

I went to a party recently, one attended by a bunch of old friends from childhood. They all seemed to have perfect lives. They are now lawyers, doctors, business owners, or on the corporate fast track, each with a spouse and two kids. All have occupations that should make mom and dad proud. It seemed that everyone was playing out the appropriate acceptable script that was set for him or her. The cars and the clothes signified to everyone else that, "Hey, I'm successful; I have money." The conversations went something like: "My kid is at Brainiac Academy" ... "I live on Envy-me Street" ... "I saw it at Saks and just couldn't resist." There were no surprises; every one was living the perfect, happy life, doing what they were supposed to do, by following the program set for them when they were children.

There is nothing wrong at all with being a physician, lawyer, or businessperson if that is truly who *YOU* want to be. My main question is: Where were the artists, the actors, the missionaries, the scholars, the scientists, and writers? Where were the people who had a passion for what they were doing in life? I suspect that they were there at the party. However, they were hidden behind masks. How many of the physicians, lawyers, business owners, or corporate clones whom we meet are actually holding these other interesting characters captive within their souls and smothering them? How many of them are not sounding their true notes, not living their lives out loud?

Prolific and best-selling author Stephen King relates to the importance of being true to your inner Self in your career. When it comes to writers deciding what to write, King says:

.."*What would be very wrong, I think I, is to turn away from what you know and like... in favor of things you believe will impress your friends, relatives, and writing circle colleagues. What's equally wrong is the deliberate turning toward some genre or type of fiction in order to make money. It's morally wonky, for one thing - the job of fiction is to find the truth inside the story's web of lies, not to commit intellectual dishonesty in the hunt for the buck.*"

Although this statement from King refers to the art of writing, it also informs us, concerning how to perform other arts -- especially the art of living life. To paraphrase King, The job of life is "to find the truth - not to commit dishonesty."

If we are not careful, trying to impress others and always hunting for the dollar can take us away from our true career and calling. In the pursuit of money and popularity, or fame and fortune, many ignore their true vocation. Some ignore their vocation to the point that they no longer feed their spirit within; therefore, their spiritual life has become weak and malnourished.

..Do you feel like a round peg in a square hole when you are at your work place? Maybe you need to be at another job or in another industry, or maybe you need to be your own boss. People stay in jobs that don't fit who they are for two reasons. Some do it out of obligation. For example, it has fallen their lot to carry on the business that dad or mom built. Most, however, do it out of fear of poverty. They know they would be happier somewhere else, but they are not willing to sacrifice a fraction of their financial security in order to make a move toward their true calling. This is a prime example of selling our souls for money.

Even if we do not change our jobs (for noble reason or bad), we should at least follow our true calling outside of our jobs. But some of us have just given up on pursuing that passion we once had. Singers stop singing, and athletes stop playing their sport. What a loss! You do not have to give up what you love just because you chose a financially secure job.

We can take care of the financial part of our lives with a well-paying job or business and investments. In a sense, if you do well in business, you can afford to truly follow your passion without the pressure of having to survive financially from your art, sport, or interest. In other words, your passion becomes your avocation, instead of your vocation. This approach at least opens an avenue that can reveal your true inner self without your having to please others. You won't be doing it for the money, and you'll be doing it outside of business hours; so, if others do not like what you are doing, then so what?

I have counseled many people who are in career paths that really don't match who they are inside. Ideally, it would be best for them to change careers. Realistically though, it can be impractical and costly for them to do so, and some of us are not willing to sell all we have and follow our Inner God. Furthermore, we have family members who depend on us to bring home the bacon. For those people who feel stuck in these careers, I try to encourage them to at least go after their passion and express themselves outside of the work place. Just because you don't get paid for it doesn't mean you still can't follow your dreams. "For what does it profit a man to gain the whole world, and forfeit his soul?" *(Mark 8:36)*

An example that comes to mind is a top insurance salesman who, at heart, is a highly skilled cabinetmaker. His free time is filled building beautiful pieces of furniture in his extensive basement workshop. In his case, his wife is delighted because she can show her husband a photograph of a rare museum piece and know that, it won't be long before she owns a splendid reproduction for their home.

Young singles are at an advantage, when it comes to career choice because they don't have spouses and usually don't have dependents, keeping them grounded in the necessities of life. The singles are freer to choose to follow their bliss - rather than the way of mammon. Unfortunately, many have been raised to consider money first in their career choices, or their experience with poverty was so painful that their focus remains on money, rather than on following their calling. Many of these young people will follow the way of materialism, not really ever getting in tune with whom they were intended to be. Ideally, young people would follow their passion and have the patience to allow that passion to produce material wealth later on.

In the words of the world renown expert on mythology, Joseph Campbell:

"I think the person who takes a job in order to live - that is to say, for the money - has turned himself into a slave. Work begins when you don't like what you are doing. There's a wise saying: make your hobby your source of income. Then there's no such thing as work, and there is no such thing as getting tired... It takes a little courage at first, because who the hell wants you to do just what you want to do; they've all got plans for you. But you can make it happen. I think it's very important for a young person to have the courage to do what seems significant in his life, and not just take a job in order to make money. But this takes a bit of prudence and very careful planning and may delay financial achievement and comfortable living. But the ultimate result will be very much to his pleasure."

If you can muster enough courage and faith in God to follow your bliss or that true Nature that is calling to you from within, you may find that the money and other things that you need and desire will follow. Earl Woods was wise enough to develop his son, Tiger's passion for golf when it was recognized at an early age. There are countless stories of great achievers in life who recognized their passion early and, rather that ignore their calling in the name of practicality and financial security, they sought first "His Kingdom and His righteousness" by embracing their passion. Then all the other things were later added to them.

How can a person expect to live a harmonious life when there is a wide internal chasm between how they live their life and the real person they are within? When we answer the inner call from God, our true vocation, by aligning ourselves with that calling, we are harmonizing ourselves to our innate design. To do otherwise, cuts against the grain of our nature. It smothers the true person and forbids him or her to live out loud. Respect your true nature, rather than deny it. To me, this is the moral of a favorite fable, "The Animal School," written by R.H. Reeves. Here is an excerpt.

Once upon a time, the animals decided they must be heroic to meet the problems of a New World," so they organized a school. They adopted an activity curriculum consisting of running, climbing, swimming and flying. To make it easier to administer, all animals took all the subjects.

The duck was excellent in swimming, better in fact than his instructor, and made excellent grades in flying, but he was very poor in running. Since he was low in running he had to stay after school and also drop swimming to practice running. This was kept up until his webfeet were badly worn, and he was only average in swimming. But average was acceptable in school, so nobody worried about that except the duck.

The rabbit started at the top of the class in running, but had a nervous breakdown because of so much make-up in swimming.

The squirrel was excellent in climbing until he developed frustrations in the flying class where his teacher made him start from the ground up instead of from the tree-top down. He also developed charley horses from over-exertion, and he got a C in climbing and a D in running.

Career Decision-making System

I've developed a career decision-making system that has been very helpful for my clients over the years. Like the sections of this book that are dedicated to finding the right love partner, the Career Decision-Making System follows *The Harmonious Way*. Whether you are in a career, ending one, or looking for one, this system can help you stay focused on creating the occupation that will add harmony to your life. If you are in a career that you are satisfied with, this system can help you appreciate your occupation as well as find problem areas. If you are in the midst of deciding whether or not to end a career, this same system can help you decide what works and doesn't work in your occupation. If you are looking for a new career, this system can keep you on track by constantly reminding you of the things that can create harmony in your life. In short, this is a beneficial three-step process to follow, no matter how happy you are or are not in your career.

Step 1: Am I a square peg in a round hole?

Square, round, triangular or whatever, there is a fit for you. To discover what type of peg you are, begin by finding some quiet time by yourself and create a list of Ideal Occupational Traits. Write the characteristics that your perfect job would have. While making your list, be as specific as possible. It will help you remember the qualities from past occupations that caused difficulties or disputes.

Here is an example:

The Harmonious Way *IDEAL JOB TRAITS*
1. Enjoy what I am doing
2. Flexible schedule
3. Located in the Southeastern USA
4. No travel involved
5. Increases my fame and recognition
6. Be my own boss.
7. No more than 48 hrs. a week
8. Express myself creatively
9. Respectable
10 Limited personal liability

Step 2: What does a square hole look like?

You've made one important list; now it's time to create another. This one is a list of Your Dream Occupations. This is a list of all the occupations you have considered pursuing in the past, as well as all of the occupations you are currently considering. List your current occupation as well to see how it compares and contrasts with others. Have fun with this list and write down not only the practical choices but the impractical ones as well.

This is, of course, just a sample list. Your list may have some or none of these characteristics on it. Also, you may have more or less. However, I believe the more the better. In any case, the important thing is to derive the list from within. This is the key to creating a harmonious lifestyle through your work. If you are true to yourself when making your list - rather than listing things that you think should be there - then your list can help you find a lifestyle that is harmonious.

Step 3: How do I find the square hole that is a good fit for me?

The next step is to juxtapose your Occupational Dream List with your Ideal Job Traits List. You do this by comparing the two lists, focusing on one occupation at a time, and asking yourself whether or not this particular occupation on the Dream List has the characteristics listed on your Job Traits list?

Though it is possible, it is not probable that you will have an occupation on your list that has all of the characteristics you listed. The important thing is to get as many of your characteristics as possible. The more characteristics that a particular occupation can provide, the more you should consider pursuing it. Score each occupation based on how well it meets your ideal job traits.

Also, let your thinking run wild. Is there an occupation that combines two of your Dream Occupations? A dentist and avid birdwatcher, who loved puttering in his workshop, got the idea that, using dental drills, he could rapidly create intricate wood carving of the feathered creatures that fascinated him so. His sideline career" soon was earning him more than his lucrative professional practice.

And, imagine someone who has multiple hobbies or interests that aren't normally thought of as careers. For example, I know of a man who loved hunting and training dogs. He didn't let that just be his pastime; he founded a national hunting dog society and built himself a well-deserved reputation as a trainer. Today the hunting world beats a path to his door to pay him for his services and advice. A person who loves to cook and entertain turned her interest into a catering service, a TV career, and the author of best-selling cookbooks. Another turned his talent and love of restoring antique cars into a six-figure income. None of these people think of themselves as having a job; however, they live quite well by seriously pursuing their hobbies." So let your imagination soar. It may take you to a new level of personal happiness and success on multiple levels.

On the next page is a sample Occupational Dream List and how to score each occupation:

The Harmonious Way *DREAM OCCUPATION SCORE*	
Present job	3/10
Job with Falcon Company	4/10
Professional Trainer	8/10
Professional Speaker	9/10
My own seminar business	9/10
Private practice	6/10
Columnist	10/10
Business partner with ABC consulting	5/10
Job with Apex Company	3/10
Business partnership with my brother-in-law	1/10

This list is an example of how you score each occupation. In the above example, the number 10 represents the number of items that were on our sample Ideal Job Trait List. Make your list as long as you like. The numerator of the fraction represents how many of the ideal traits that particular occupation provides. The higher the fraction, the closer it is to the number 1, the better. One represents an integrated whole, which is our goal. On this list the columnist occupation scored the highest, and then the professional speaker and trainer occupations followed. Based on this sample list, the person who created it should seriously consider leaving her or his present job and focus on one of these high scoring occupations because the higher scoring jobs can provide more fulfillment and satisfaction.

Are you looking for a career? If so, here's a suggestion: keep your lists in a folder and put the folder somewhere you visit everyday, such as a desk or nightstand drawer. Read it frequently. Make sure you fill out your lists in pencil because they are subject to change. You can add and subtract from them at will. You may discover that certain job traits you thought were important to you are actually not or that job traits you did not consider important actually are. These lists attract your ideal career to you. This happens because the more you read, edit, and review it, the more mental energy you are devoting to it. The more mental energy you devote to it, the more you send out vibrations to the universe that manipulate the physical ethos to bend to your will. This is the power of thought. To think is to create. Yes, it really works.

When job opportunities arise, evaluate them based on how they measure up to your Ideal Job Traits List. I stress this because, depending on your particular situation, there are times when the thought of a high or secure salary can seriously tempt you to take a job that's not right for you. Have you ever disregarded the Holy Spirit within and taken a job - even though you knew it wasn't right for you? If so, my guess is that it did not work out just as you had anticipated.

I have counseled people who have told me they knew from the start that they were not in the right career; however, they were financially poor or desperate or just going along with the social pressure. Deep down they knew they were deliberately selecting a career path they didn't want to follow. Consequently, they faced a life of "what could have been," rather than fulfilling lives. What stood in the way of their finding their rightful place in the universe was being dishonest with themselves from the beginning.

So, be honest with yourself. Risk planning to live your life out loud, sounding your own true note. Share your hopes and dreams with those in your life who are in harmony with you. You may find their ideas, suggestions, and contacts could help you follow *The Harmonious Way* to happier, more rewarding relationships in all aspects of your life.

About The Author

AARON TURPEAU is a professional counselor and relationship expert who lectures nationally on personal growth, spiritual development and interpersonal relationships. He has a M.Div. from the School of Theology at Claremont and a M.Ed. and a Ph.D. in Psychology from the University of Georgia. Dr. Turpeau is a licensed counselor in the state of Georgia and has been an Instructor of Religion at Morehouse College since 1999.

He is a member of the American Counseling Association, the International Association of Marriage and Family Counselors, and the Society for Human Resource Management.

Dr. Turpeau is currently president of Turpeau Enterprises, a corporation dedicated to personal growth. He lives in Northern Georgia with his wife, Michelle, and three children. He and Michelle and have been harmoniously married since 1992.

If you would like to share with me ways in which you create harmony and joy in your life, e-mail me at aaron@drturpeau.com

To Order *The Harmonious Way* you may :

- Order at your local bookstore by supplying them with **ISBN: 0-9725934-0-3**.

- Or visit my website,

www.drturpeau.com